By Bruce Jay Friedman

SCUBA DUBA (*play*)
BLACK ANGELS (*stories*)
A MOTHER'S KISSES
FAR FROM THE CITY OF CLASS (*stories*)
STERN

SCUBA

DUBA

A TENSE COMEDY BY

Bruce Jay Friedman

SIMON AND SCHUSTER · NEW YORK

First Printing

LIBRARY OF CONGRESS CATALOG CARD NUMBER: 68–19941
DESIGNED BY EVE METZ
MANUFACTURED IN THE UNITED STATES OF AMERICA
BOOK PRESS, NEW YORK, N.Y.

Scuba Duba was presented by Ivor David Balding in association with Alvin Ferleger and Gordon Crowe for The Establishment Theatre Company at the New Theatre, New York City, on October 10, 1967. Staged by Jacques Levy. Setting by Peter Larkin. Costumes by Willa Kim. Lighting by Jules Fisher. Music by Stanley Walden.

THE CAST

HAROLD WONDER	Jerry Orbach
CAROL JANUS	Brenda Smiley
TOURIST	Conrad Bain
LANDLADY	Rita Karin
VOICE OF HAROLD'S MOTHER	Stella Longo
GENDARME	Bernard Poulain
THIEF	Judd Hirsch
DR. SCHOENFELD	Ken Olfson
CHEYENNE	Christine Norden
JEAN WONDER	Jennifer Warren
FOXTROT (FROGMAN)	Cleavon Little
REDDINGTON	Rudy Challenger

SETTING

The main room of a château in southern France. The present.

Photographs of the
Original Production

Harold Wonder "*just calling his mother.*"

ALL PHOTOGRAPHS BY BERT ANDREWS

The Thief bewailing his lot in life, encouraged by the
Gendarme and the Landlady, while Harold and Miss
Janus look on, bewildered.

Harold and Miss Janus trying to wrest Harold's muffler from Dr. Schoenfeld and Cheyenne.

Harold receiving help from Dr. Schoenfeld.

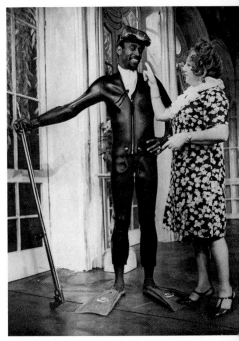

The Landlady "recognizing" Foxtrot as Sidney Poitier.

Miss Janus distracting Harold.

Jean Wonder and Reddington standing by as Harold attacks Foxtrot.

Jean Wonder and Miss Janus getting to know one another.

Harold making a last attempt to prevent his wife Jean from leaving with Reddington.

ACT ONE

ACT I

SCENE: Main room of château. South of France. Early evening. Young man, thirty-five or thereabout, visibly upset, paces back and forth. He wears a bathrobe, pajamas, slippers, and holds a large gardener's scythe, but seems unaware it exists. Someone is playing a piano in a neighboring house, something loud, abrasive, in the style of Khachaturian's "Sabre Dance." He goes to the window, looks toward the source of the music.

HAROLD WONDER: I really needed this. This is exactly what I came here for. (HE opens the window and gestures with the scythe, calling out at the same time) Hello! Hey!

(Music stops, a young girl, quite pretty, and wearing a bikini, appears)

MISS JANUS: Hi.

HAROLD: Hey. Thanks for dropping in. I'm not allowed to leave, myself. (Defensively) I don't need anyone's permission. It's just better if I stay here.

MISS JANUS: I thought you might have a giant bird flying loose around here and called me over to help. Every few months someone does that to me. I seem to give the impression I'd know what to do about people's loose birds.

HAROLD (*Distantly*): I wish that's all it was. I wish I could turn the whole thing into a bird problem. (*Coming back*) I thought you'd look different. I thought you'd be a little, I don't know, a little noisier-looking. (HE *has been using the scythe to accompany his speech*) Oh this? I'm sorry. I just picked it up and started carrying it around. Well, I didn't just pick it up. Actually, we had a prowler a few nights ago. My wife opened the shutters and came face to face with him, some kind of Swede she said it was. With a frying pan on his head.

MISS JANUS (*Making herself at home*): Maybe he just wanted to go through your wife's purse. Not to steal anything, but just to see what was in it. I had a Syrian friend once who loved to do that. We had a thing where I'd fill up my purse, pretend to be asleep, and then he'd tiptoe in and go through it. I put all kinds of surprises in there for him—birth control pills, religious ornaments, surgical appliances, pictures of other Syrian guys . . .

HAROLD: I don't think he was after any of that. I think he was after much bigger stuff. Look, I'm here with my wife. Except for the slight problem that I'm suddenly not here with my wife. That she decided not to be here. (*Gesturing with scythe*) On that prowler I mentioned, it doesn't show, but I'm actually big enough under these things to take care of any trouble by myself. (*Referring to scythe*) It's just something I do. Whenever there's trouble I pick up things. A friend of mine and I once started a little fight, just for fun. Before we began, I remember unconsciously picking up a chicken. One of those ready-made roasted things. I wasn't going to use it or anything. You can imagine how much good it would do you in a fight.

Fly all over the goddamned place. I just seem to need something in my hands.

MISS JANUS: You're probably a very tactile person. I am, too. (SHE *gets up and flicks at her bikini bottom*) Listen, does this fit or doesn't it? I bought it today and there were some German girls who said it was too small and I was hanging out of it. They could only speak about four words of English, but they managed to get that much across. (*In imitation of German accent*) "Madame . . . from the bottom . . . you are too wide . . ." (*Resuming normal style*) They'd been trying on bikinis and theirs didn't fit, so it may be they were just trying to spoil mine. The proprietor said it was because they were from Düsseldorf. Düsseldorf girls try them on all day long and never buy them. That must be some city—Düsseldorf.

HAROLD: Look, I don't want to know Düsseldorf. I'm in the middle of something awful. Something that's really ripping me up. That happened tonight. But I just want you to know that your suit fits. Right out of my terribleness I know it fits. I never saw anything fit like that in my entire life.

MISS JANUS: I wish I could get to the state where I truly believed my behind was beautiful.

HAROLD: That's always a big breakthrough.

MISS JANUS: Want me to tell you something I've never told anyone in my whole life. I was working in a place in the Village when I first came to New York. They had an ad that said they only wanted girls who looked like Modigliani paintings. Well, I was *feeling* kind of Modigliani-ish, so I went over and I got the job. It was a little disappointing. I was expecting hippies, acid heads, flower-power . . . It turned out to be a hangout for electricians. Well, there were five guys with long hair who at least *looked* a little Villagey and I'd pretend they were exotic types even though they kept talking about—what are those electric things?

HAROLD: Volts? Amperes?

MISS JANUS: That's the one, amperes. For a couple of weeks they never really said anything to me except "Another Cappuccino." And then one morning—can you imagine, it was broad daylight—they said they'd like to take some pictures of me. Even then I knew what kind of pictures they meant. When I was off at eleven, I said, very business-like, "Okay, I'll go with you and take a few . . ." (*Trails off as though the story is over*)

HAROLD (*Completely hooked*): So?

MISS JANUS: Oh! So I followed them to a brownstone and we started off with some madonna-like portraits and then, because I really knew what it was all about, I took off all my clothes without them even asking. And that was just for openers. They started moving the camera around and I started moving myself around and I was carrying on as though I were in a trance. I don't know how long it took, but then I heard a ship's horn in the harbor and I put on my clothes and went home.

HAROLD: Did you . . .

MISS JANUS: . . . Sleep with them? No. I'm not sure really whether I wanted to or whether I would have. But I didn't.

HAROLD: That's some story. I loved it and everything, but that's some story. You just walked in here and sat down and I'm your neighbor and that's the kind of story you tell? I did love it, though. I hated it and I loved it.

MISS JANUS: I know. I did, too. I hated it and I loved it and I knew you would too. I could tell.

HAROLD: Look, I'm in bad trouble. You remember that wife I mentioned earlier? She pulled something real cute on me. If I wasn't so embarrassed I'd be shaking like a leaf. I've got two kids sleeping upstairs. Until you came over I'd just been calling up people. I tried to get Dr. Schoenfeld in Monaco. Thank God, I thought of him.

MISS JANUS: Don't tell me. He's your analyst.

HAROLD: Uh-uh. I don't fool around with that stuff. He's just a guy I know who lives in my building and happens to be a psychiatrist. I talk to him a lot in elevators and I seem to just bump into him in haberdashery shops, places like that. It's the most extraordinary thing. All he has to do is say three words to me and I feel better.

(Cut-out of DR. SCHOENFELD appears)

I was fired from a job once. It was a big argument over whether I was allowed to use the executive john. Later I started to make more money than ever—but the idea of being fired was wiping me out. So Dr. Schoenfeld says . . .

DR. SCHOENFELD'S VOICE: You're good at looking up and down, Harold, but you've never once looked at life sideways . . .

HAROLD: . . . I never once looked at life sideways. He was suggesting I start looking at my problems out of the corner of my eye. It doesn't sound like much, but I tried it . . . (*Demonstrating*) You know, there's a hell of a lot going on over there on the sides.

(DR. SCHOENFELD'S *cut-out disappears*)

I have to call him in a little while. Look, I feel much better now, even though that electrician story of yours got me a little nervous. I feel like a damned fool about why I called you over in the first place.

MISS JANUS: You probably wanted to borrow something.

HAROLD: Well, actually, it was the piano. It was getting me jumpy. But now that I've met you, I'm sure it wouldn't bother me. You can play all you like.

MISS JANUS: It's nice when you look at my eyes. I just realized that hardly anyone ever does that. People look at my lips, my neck, my feet . . .

HAROLD: That's what I was doing? I was looking at your eyes? The trouble was I didn't know who was playing. It might have been anyone. But now that I know you're friendly, you can bang away to your heart's content.

MISS JANUS: Say, what do you do?

HAROLD: I'm in billboards. I write the stuff on them.

MISS JANUS: I'll bet you're great at it.

HAROLD: About three years ago some Bennington girl wrote an essay for the *Partisan Review* that said the prose on my billboards was the true urban folk literature of the sixties, much more important than Faulkner . . . (*Considers this, clucks his head as though to say "Can you imagine anything that farfetched?"*) Look, I'm expecting these phone calls. But really, you can do anything you like. You can burn incense if you like and blow it into my chimney. I mean you've gotten me through a little piece of the night and that's the whole deal. If I can just make it through to the morning I'll be able to handle things a little better.

(HAROLD WONDER'S LANDLADY, *a French woman, slightly past middle age, enters with a prospective* CLIENT *for the house—presumably for the month after the* WONDERS *vacate.* CLIENT *is an American, middle-aged, robust*)

TOURIST: Well, I like it. It's French. And you can tell it's French. It smells French. I mean the goddamned air is French. As long as you're going to be in the country I think you ought to just jump in and French it up. Like these salesgirls. Cute little biscuits, but did you ever get a whiff of them. Now ordinarily I'd haul off and tell them what I think of them, but what the hell, you're in France. I just let them go ahead and stink up the place. It's their country.

LANDLADY: Excuse me, I was just showing the château for when you leave. (*To* MISS JANUS) You are in the films, no?

MISS JANUS: No. (*Leaving*)

LANDLADY: You're not in the films?

MISS JANUS: No.

LANDLADY (*To* TOURIST): She's in the films.

MISS JANUS: 'Bye.

(SHE *leaves*)

LANDLADY: Au revoir, mademoiselle . . . I know that face . . .
(*To* TOURIST) Françoise Sagan has had this house. Charles
Aznavour. Brigitte Bardot was down for the summer with
Jacques Tati. We have had Irving de Gaulle.

TOURIST: Irving de Gaulle?

LANDLADY: He is a brother of Charles, but he stays very quiet.
They say he tells Charles exactly what to do, but in a
whisper so no one will know. I myself have heard him pick
up the phone in this very house and tell his brother to,
how you say, screw Algeria. (*Turning to* HAROLD) Excuse
me, monsieur. We are through in five seconds. (*To the*
TOURIST) Monsieur Wonder is here because at the last
second your Steve McQueen called to say he could not
make it.

HAROLD: It's a little late.

TOURIST: Now that's the kind of talk I like. It's late and you
just came right out and said it was late. It's not *that* late,
actually, but that's not what I'm getting at. I think you
ought to call a thing what it is. I got this guy works for
me and he's bald, see. Oh, he's got a little swirl of a thing

sitting back there on his head and he kind of brings it forward, but for Christ's sake, the man is a skinhead, no two ways about it. Well, I could putter around and pretend I don't even notice it, you know, kind of kid him along. But I don't, see. He comes into my office every morning with a report and I don't let two minutes go by before I say "Hey there, Small"—that's his name—"I see you're parting your hair in the middle." Now he chokes up a little and I'm not about to say that he eats it up exactly —but for Christ's sake, I've laid the thing right out on the table instead of pretending it's not there. And, of course, to spare his feelings I've kind of blended it in with a little humor, which I believe in doing. The parting your hair in the middle part. That's humorous. It's not like I said "Get your tail in here, you bald son of a bitch" or anything. They do that in some offices. But I kind of skirt around the edges. That's how I keep my employees. You got a Chink's around here?

LANDLADY: Monsieur?

TOURIST: A Chinese restaurant.

HAROLD: There's a Vietnamese place around five miles down the road.

TOURIST: As long as they got those eggrolls I don't care what kind of Chink they are. I been all over the world, but I can't really settle into a place unless I know there's a good Chink's nearby. I understand they're opening them up all over Moscow. We got one in my town, a kind of drive-in Chink's. Night he opened up I was first in line. I said to him "You're pretty goddamned lucky to be here, buster." He looked kind of puzzled, but he knew damned well what I was talking about. I said to him "Let's say the dice had taken an extra roll. You could have been over there in Shanghai someplace starving to death." They got four-year-old prostitutes over there, I understand. Girl gets to be eight and she's still got her cherry, old Mao Tse-tung gives her a goddamned peace prize. You know what I'm talking about. "You'd have had beri-beri by now if you'd been over there. So you just keep those eggrolls *hot*, Mr. Chinkhead, and everything'll be all right." . . . We never had any trouble with the guy. Hell, for all I know he could have been a *citizen* or something, but that gets us right to my philosophy. Lay it on the line.

HAROLD (*To* LANDLADY, *temper snapping*): Look, in case anyone forgot, this is my house until September first. I'm not interested in any Elks' Convention. Would you mind just clearing out of here. I've got some calls coming and I'd like a little privacy.

TOURIST: That's all right, son, that's frank talk. We're not really intruding, the way I see it, but you think we are and you said so. No need to apologize. I like it here. I think I'll take it. It's French. Got a little of that salesgirl smell to it. (*Leaving*) Take it easy, son, and don't take any wooden frogs' legs.

(TOURIST exists)

LANDLADY: Ah, wonderful. I call Charlton Heston immediately and tell him sorry the house is rented. (*Writing in a little book*) Alors, that takes care of September. He is charming, non? I think he is a famous actor.

HAROLD: For Christ's sake, he's *not* a famous actor.

LANDLADY: No, no, I am never wrong about these things. I think he is Tony Curtis. Yes, I'm sure of it. Tony would not want to make a big fuss over it, you know how they are. I notice madame is not here. (*Primping*)

HAROLD: You notice goddamned right.

LANDLADY (*Seductively, humming a little romantic refrain*): When I was a girl I was the fairest flower in all Provence. They would come from miles around to gaze at me. And when there was a man I admired, my petals would open, one by one—floop, floop, floop.

HAROLD: Look, that's the last thing I want to hear about right now.

LANDLADY: And I have a secret for you, monsieur. My petals still open, not as often perhaps, but wider than ever.

HAROLD: Look, madame, I'm sure you were a winner in the old days and that you're still standing room only. But don't you see I'm a wreck? . . . Anyway, how come you didn't do anything when I shouted last night?

LANDLADY: You mean when we had the prowler?

HAROLD: When *I* had the prowler. I had to look in the guide-book to find out how to yell for help. Didn't you hear me? *Au secours, au secours!* I felt like a goddamned jackass.

LANDLADY (*Correcting pronunciation*): Se-cours. Ours. Say! *Se-Cours!*

HAROLD (*Trying it*): Secours.

LANDLADY: That is much better. What about the police, monsieur?

HAROLD: Oh sure, I know about the police. I got a cop on the phone and explained what happened. He said the only way he'd come is if I drove over there and watched the station for him. They've got one cop for the whole god-damned South of France. Look, madame, I appreciate your company. I really do. But I'm in terrible trouble and I'm expecting these phone calls. I can't really talk when any-one's around. When I was a teenager I'd have to take all my calls in the closet. I'd put all these overcoats over my head. It's the only way I feel private.

LANDLADY: All right, monsieur, I understand. But remember that madame has a special cure for young men. The won-ders of France. Your Jimmy Cagney was in such trouble. He comes to madame and poof, he wins the Oscar.

> (SHE *leaves.* HE *smokes, putters around nervously, looks at phone, decides against it. Goes to window with scythe. Opens shutters, hollers out* au secours, au secours—*first loudly, then breaking off into a plain-tive cry. Phone rings.* HE *picks it up, still holding scythe*)

HAROLD: New York? Yes, operator, I'll take it.

> (Cut-out of MOTHER appears)

Hello, Mom.

MOTHER'S VOICE: Is that you, Harold?

HAROLD: Yeah, Mom, all the way from France.

MOTHER'S VOICE: What happened, sweetheart?

HAROLD: Nothing, Mom, nothing at all. I just decided to call. But I'll have to make it fast because it's costing a god-damned fortune. I don't even know how much. Oh Christ, I can't concentrate. It's too expensive.

MOTHER'S VOICE: First tell me about the children, sweetheart.

HAROLD: They're fine.

MOTHER'S VOICE: And is it nice in France?

HAROLD: It's wonderful, Mom. A wonderful country.

MOTHER'S VOICE: Harold, you have something heavy in your hand, don't you?

HAROLD (*Looking at scythe, then dropping it*): How the hell did you know that?

MOTHER'S VOICE: I've been your mother for a long time, darling.

HAROLD: Jesus, it must have cost a grand already and I haven't even said anything. Look, Ma, I'm in lousy trouble, so I'm just calling up people. I just want it to hurry up and be tomorrow morning.

MOTHER'S VOICE: Something did happen to the children. I knew it.

HAROLD: No, Mom. I told you they're fine.

MOTHER'S VOICE: Is your wife at your side—where she belongs?

HAROLD: No, Mom, Jean is out. That's what it's all about.

MOTHER'S VOICE: I knew it. I could have predicted the whole thing. Who is she out with, darling?

HAROLD: Mom, I can hardly get it out of my mouth. She's run off with a spade frogman.

MOTHER'S VOICE: What kind of frogman, darling?

HAROLD: A spade. Don't you know what that is? She's run off with a goddamned black scuba diver!

MOTHER'S VOICE: Don't talk that way, Harold. It's not nice.

HAROLD: All right, Mom. She's with a dark-skinned phantom of the ocean depths. Is that better? How do you think I feel saying something like that on the phone and you don't think I said it politely enough?

MOTHER'S VOICE (*Still calm, although news is sinking in now*): A colored frogman. That's what she needed, a colored frogman. You know why she's doing that, don't you, Harold? Because you didn't do enough for her. None of us did. The whole family didn't strip itself naked enough for her. And what did you give her, Harold? The French Riviera? That isn't a vacation, darling, that's a punishment. Didn't you know that? That's where you take people instead of throwing them into dungeons. You know where I would have taken her, Harold. I would have brought her back to that ghetto in Baltimore where you found her on the streets!

HAROLD (*Interrupting*): Look, now don't go too far. You're not exactly a bargain yourself, you know!

MOTHER'S VOICE: Harold, I think there's something wrong with the connection. You couldn't possibly have said what I just heard you say.

HAROLD: How about that cello player you took me up to see when I was seven years old? You forgot him, eh? And that guy who made those alligator handbags. Never heard of him, eh? Well, I didn't forget them so easy. It didn't exactly do me any good to be in on that stuff, so don't go picking on Jean.

MOTHER'S VOICE: Is that why you called, Harold? You thought your mother needed a little filth thrown in her face. All the way from France.

HAROLD: All right, Mom, I'm sorry. I didn't mean to get into that.

MOTHER'S VOICE (*In tears*): That's all right, Harold. I'll just consider that my payment after thirty-six years of being your mother.

HAROLD: I think she's going to stay out the whole night and I'm not sure I can take it. I'm waiting for a call now. I'm all alone here.

MOTHER'S VOICE: Harold, you know what your mother's going to do now? She's going to quietly take a boat and she's coming right over to France.

HAROLD: All right, all right. I'm calm now. Look, I have to say goodbye. This call is costing around twelve grand already.

MOTHER'S VOICE: And you promise me you'll use your head?

HAROLD: I promise. But if you hear the phone again from France, don't get nervous.

MOTHER'S VOICE: Believe me, sweetheart, you forget, but I've been through much worse than this. A mother doesn't forget. Much worse, Harold. This is a little nothing.

HAROLD: I know, Mom. There's just something about her staying out all night in a foreign country. Listen, are you sure you're okay?

MOTHER'S VOICE: Wonderful, Harold. I saw this Virginia Woolf they're all raving about. Frankly, I wouldn't give you two cents for Elizabeth Taylor!

HAROLD: I got to go now, Mom.

MOTHER'S VOICE: Goodbye, darling.

> (THEY exchange half a dozen goodbyes; finally HAROLD hangs up, cutting her off in the middle of one, and MOTHER cut-out disappears)

HAROLD: That was a fast eighty-seven dollars for a goodbye. I don't care. I'll talk to myself. What do I care? There's no law. As long as it makes me feel better, that's the only thing. (Goes to window. Shouting) Jeannie, you bitch. France you picked to pull this on me. Not in Queens where I have defenses. Where I have friends. (Plaintively) Au secours, au secours. (Hears piano playing, sweet, melodic) That's okay. That's fine. It doesn't bother me any more. Now that I know she's friendly . . . It's one of my favorite mazurkas. (Goes to the window and yells out) You can play it all night if you like. (Music stops)

(MISS JANUS *appears, still in bikini, eating from a fruit bowl*)

MISS JANUS: Hi, could you hear me playing? I came over to find out.

HAROLD: No. I mean, I could, but it was fine.

MISS JANUS: Want some fruit? Make you strong.

HAROLD: I couldn't get anything down.

MISS JANUS (*Eating away*): It's like eating pure strength. I'm not fooling.

HAROLD: I never saw anyone eat fruit like that. You're kind of slopping it up and eating your fingers right along with it, and what is it? It's wonderful. (*Switching*) Look, I'm in all this trouble. You probably guessed it's about my wife. And this colored scuba diver. (*Chanting louder and louder*) Scuba duba duba. Scuba duba duba. Scuba duba duba. That's what keeps bouncing through my head.

(*Cut-out of giant ape-man appears for a moment. Jungle drums are heard. Cut-out disappears.*)

MISS JANUS: You really are upset. Would you like me to cradle your head?

HAROLD: What do you mean?

MISS JANUS (*Making a cradling gesture at her bosom*): In here. Sometimes that's all people need, people with the world's toughest exteriors.

HAROLD (*Trying it but unable really to fit into a good cradle*): I don't think I'm doing it right. Anyway, it's hard to just sail into one of those.

MISS JANUS: All right, but if at any time you feel the need . . . just signal me. (SHE *demonstrates with cradling pantomime*) And we'll start right in, no formalities . . .

HAROLD: Okay, but meanwhile, if I start acting funny, just shove a little applesauce into me. It's in the kitchen. If you can just be with me awhile.

MISS JANUS: I can stay as long as you like. I was just château-sitting for my friend Abby and her new husband. Abby and I were roommates in New York while she was going with him. He's a sculptor named Nero. For three years she couldn't even get him to *talk* about marriage—until two months ago when she had her left breast removed. Suddenly Nero felt responsible as hell, wanted to marry her immediately. She hadn't come out of the ether and he had her in front of a minister. Abby wouldn't let me move out—it was almost as though she felt sorry for me for having both my breasts and having to be single. So I kind of tagged along with them to France. Something's supposed to happen between the three of us. I'm not sure what. It hasn't yet, but it's always in the air. At least once a day someone says "What'll we do tonight?" Then the air gets very tense. I think it would have happened already, but no one knows how to start. Or who's supposed to do what to who. And then there's always Abby's breast to worry about. How are you supposed to work that in?

HAROLD (*Abashed*): You walked in here with some collection of stories . . .

MISS JANUS: Maybe some night Nero will say "Let's go, girls" and we'll all take off our clothes. Simple as that.

HAROLD (*Looking out shutters*): You know, my wife's got the goddamned car. What am I supposed to do, take a taxi to Marseille, get out and say, "Pardon me, did you see this American woman and this black person with flippers on his feet?" He wears them out of the water, right on the goddamned sidewalk! He's graceful in them too, that's the awful part. Got one of those Jean Paul Belmondo styles. I mean what am I supposed to do, say he looks like W. C. Fields just because he's out jazzing my wife and I'm here with two kids trying to get through the goddamned night? I'm sorry. Please go on.

MISS JANUS: I think what's supposed to happen is that Abby is going to die and then Nero and I are logically supposed to more or less blend together. Say a month or so later. None of us have ever said it, but you guess that's what it's all about. We're waiting for Abby to die. He's very attractive and everything, but I wish he'd really wait. Like yesterday, Abby was out at the beach somewhere gathering shells—she gets beautiful ones now, the most exquisite you've ever seen, almost as though they've been left for her because she's going to die. He came up behind me, put his hands very deliberately on my two breasts almost as though he was counting them, and asked me to inhale something he keeps in a sponge. Well, all it does is make my behind itch a little. I've taken them all—pot, mescaline, LSD—I get a little sleepy and then my behind itches.

HAROLD: Look, there's something you ought to know.

MISS JANUS: Yes?

HAROLD: I'm a married man. (*Chuckling ironically*) Some married. You know, she's had a series of these guys, not really *had* them as far as I know, but all one of them has to be is slightly worthless and she gets turned right on.

(*Cut-outs of* THREE MEN *appear in the room: one with floor-waxing equipment, a second in trunks with a swimming pool vacuum, and a third with a garbage man's trash sticker*)

The first one was a floor shellacker, then there was this guy who cleaned up swimming pools in Barbados. So help me, Christ, there was a garbage collector in Baltimore. He was a little classier than the rest of the garbage crowd. He'd only handle metal and wood. Left the mushy stuff to the other boys, but he was a garbage man all right, no matter how you slice it. It's a classical kind of deal. She can only relax with a man when she feels he isn't worth four cents. If he knows the alphabet he's finished.

(*Cut-outs of* THREE MEN *disappear, arms locked in camaraderie*)

I once tried acting a little low-down myself. I started hanging around the house in these Puerto Rican clothes. So one day Jeannie reached into my jacket and grabbed this extra inch of fat I have around my waist and wouldn't let go—she was letting me know who I was, underneath all the clothes. She wouldn't let go until I hit her. Came down hard on one of her pressure points. There's one in there, right around the shoulder blades. I used to memorize lists of pressure points and erogenous zones . . . (*Switching*) Listen, why the hell don't you just move away from your friends?

MISS JANUS: I've drifted in with them and I don't seem to be able to drift out. It's that drifting I can't get over. It was that way the first time too. Men like to hear about the first time. I was going with a boy and my father didn't really like him so one night he pointed a gun at the boy's head and went "Pow." Like a joke. Only I got very nauseous and the next thing I knew the boy and I were drifting out to the highway and we sort of drifted into this shed that was full of old magazines and newspapers from all over the world. I let him make love to me right in the middle of all those publications. I can still remember their names. (*Closing her eyes, and in a sort of religious chant, enunciating each one very deliberately*) The Philadelphia *Bulletin*, the Des Moines *Register*, the *Deutschlander Verlag, Paris-Soir,* the Sacramento *Bee,* the Newark *Star-Ledger, Variety,* the *Bulletin of Atomic Scientists* . . .

HAROLD: You know, I really love the kind of stories you tell, the kind where those things happen to you. Look, I don't know what's going to happen, you're terribly attractive, the way you eat fruit, for example, but I'm in the middle of this thing. (*Hollering out window*) Come on out and fight, you black son of a bitch. Jeannie, I dare you to produce him now that I know what his game is! (*To* MISS JANUS) I don't even know my own name. I've got these kids asleep upstairs. But couldn't we have this thing together in which you just tell me those stories—even if nothing else happens? They kind of sneak up on me— like a hug or something.

MISS JANUS: They never worked on Juan.

HAROLD: All right, let me sit down for this one. I'm sitting down for Juan.

MISS JANUS: He was just an eight-year-old boy in a slum school where I worked as a substitute teacher. Everyone in the whole school had tried to get through to him—but he kept on being sullen and withdrawn, wouldn't say a word, wouldn't meet your eyes. So then I took a crack at him. I told him all these stories. And at the end he was just as sullen and withdrawn as before.

HAROLD: That's the whole Juan story? That's what I sat down for? Look, I'll tell you quite frankly—I didn't like the material in that one. But I liked every one up to now. I love them even though they wreck me. I mean did you see me at the window with that black son of a bitch routine? Well, it's true. I really would like to run this thing . . . (*Gesturing with scythe*) . . . right through his gizzard. But look, let's face it, you know the type of fellow I am— the straightest guy in France, right? Well, the truth is, I encouraged the whole thing. Just the way I'm getting you to tell those stories. What happened is that we met the black bastard in Cannes one afternoon, right after we got here, standing around at one of those sidewalk restaurants, with his flippers on and this black suit and that breathing equipment on his back. Wait a minute. (*Goes to slide machine*) You want to hear something? I even took pictures of the goddamn thing. (*As he is pulling a very long screen out of a very small closet*) Longest closet in France. (*Sets up slide show*) Take a seat. Any seat in the house. (MISS JANUS *complies. First slide of* FROGMAN *comes into focus*) There he is . . . Now, you take away the skindiving stuff and he isn't really that handsome, but he has this smile that shows up now and then. It's as though he has a zipper across his mouth. He kind of unzips that smile and when you see his teeth it kind of puts him a different league. . . . Anyway, all summer long we'd been hearing

about this wonderful loup fish, and Jeannie, who's one of
the original fish-eaters, was really starved for one. Well,
the restaurant was sorry but it was fresh out. So that's
when this skindiver guy comes over to the table. I don't
know whether he'd heard us or not, but the next thing
you know, he goes flying over to the pier and heaves himself into the water, and I'll be goddamned if he doesn't
come up with one of those loup fish on the end of his
spear! "Voilà babe! Compliments of Stokely Carmichael,
the Honorable Martin Luther King and Cab Calloway."
Well, it really was a kind of charming thing to do. I
mean the way he presented the damned thing. Anyway,
we bought him a drink, dinner. He didn't say much except
that even as a kid he'd always had these strong lungs.
(Goes up to FROGMAN's image on screen, shouts) Come
on out you son of a bitch. I'll take you on even if you
have got strong lungs and I am a little afraid of that speargun. (Climbs down as though nothing happened) Well,
actually, he didn't seem like a bad guy, we didn't know
anybody . . . So the next thing I know, Jeannie and I are
in Cannes again and I find myself saying "Let's go see
old Scuba Duba." All my own idea. I have to say that
for Jeannie. So far she hadn't even taken a good look at
him. I was the mastermind—really brilliant the way I
served him up, just like a bowl of strawberries. The way
I planned it, a real Normandy Invasion. I smoked him out
that second time. It wasn't easy—he was out working on
shrimp boats or something—but I found him and for the
next week we just went around together. I even took him
along when we went to get her hair set. (Rips out one of
the slides and tears it up) One thing I resent is paying
for all those drinks, you bastard, and this has nothing to
do with your being black, so don't get any ideas. (Closes
up slide equipment) So next thing I know, she insists on

being by herself one afternoon, and then a second time, a few more times, and then I get this call earlier tonight. This is it, she says. I'm with him, I'm staying with him and it isn't just for tonight, it's for always, words and music by Irving Berlin. I can go down to the Mediterranean and drain it out cup by cup as far as she's concerned and it's not going to do any good. I'm supposed to stay with the children and maybe she'll call and at a certain point she'll come and get them because she wants them. And she's not kidding either, this really *is* it. You should have heard her voice. So what am I supposed to do now, ask some spade if I can come visit my kids once in a while? Work my ass off so she can buy gold flippers for a goddamned spade frogman? What's he gonna do, send my kids to some spade school? A spade underwater school in France somewhere? (*In mock imitation*) "Now you take the flippers in one hand . . ." What am I supposed to do, start calling up girls now and ask them out on picnics? In the condition I'm in? What do I do, go to Over Twenty-eight dances? I mean, what the hell am I supposed to do? I'm shaking like a leaf. How do you feel about men crying?

MISS JANUS: It's all right. I don't have any special theories about it. I have a feeling it would be all right if you did it.

HAROLD: I'll just turn around here for a second and try to get it over with as soon as possible. (*Turns head*) That ought to do it. It wasn't too bad, was it?

MISS JANUS: You have a beautiful neck.

HAROLD: Really? It's big, but I never thought much about it being beautiful. What a nice thing to say. I mean, if you said I was handsome that's one thing, but when you compliment a neck you've got to be serious.

MISS JANUS: What happened then?

HAROLD: Maybe I ought to show it off a little more. (*Switches*) Well, first I thought I'd get her back by insulting him. "You think you're going to be able to shop at Bendel's on what he makes with those flippers? What do you think is down at the bottom of that French ocean anyway? There's just a bunch of French shit down there. And back in the States, what'll you do, go to Freedom Marches together? Eat hominy grits? Sit around and read back issues of *Ebony*?" Well, I didn't get very far with that approach. So then I switched over to all the things we'd had together over the eight years, and you know I couldn't come up with very much. The sex you can forget about. You see, one time, when we were just married, she looked up while we were making love and saw my hand up in the air. "What's that?" she asked. "It's my hand," I said. "Well, what's it *doing* up there?" she asked. "Where's it supposed to be?" I asked. "Well, shouldn't it be *doing* something?" she said. Well, I said, the other hand was *doing* something, but she didn't see it that way and it was kind of downhill ever since then. Now the only time she gets excited is in bathrooms at other people's houses.

MISS JANUS: I never tried that. I'm not knocking it or anything. But it's funny.

HAROLD: Yeah. She goes into the toilet and she pulls me in there with her and she's as hot as a snake. All our friends know by now. We go to a party, they all stand around waiting for us to come out. Believe me, that's no sex life.

So I tried to think of some other stuff and all I could come up with was a trip to Quebec we once took. "What about that trip to Quebec?" I said to her. "What about it?" she said. "Well, wasn't it something?" "It wasn't that great," she said. I said, "Yeah, but didn't we see a ship from Israel at the waterfront that wasn't even supposed to be there?" She agreed we saw a ship from Israel, but that was no reason to keep a marriage together. I had to agree with her there. So then there wasn't much else I could do except hit her with the kids. Well, this Negro gentleman friend of hers was way ahead of me on that. He told her the kids were going to be fine, she said. Yeah. "Well, maybe that's in colored divorces," I said, "but my kids aren't going to be fine. (*Hollering out window*) Not with any goddamned spade frogman stepfather." I love my kids. I have this one game I play with them. I got to show you. It's called "Can't Get Out."

MISS JANUS: What do I do?

HAROLD: Oh, just pretend you're Jamie. I say to you "Now I'm going to get you in one of the toughest grips known to the Western World. It's called the 'Double Reverse Panther Bear Pretzel Twist.' No man in history has ever been known to get out of this grip. Are you ready? Do you dare to allow me to get you into it?"

MISS JANUS: I do.

HAROLD: I do, Daddy.

MISS JANUS: I do, Daddy.

HAROLD: Well, then I spend a long time getting them into it. This kind of thing. (*Twists her around, this way and that, tying up her arms, legs)* "Okay," I say, "now you're in it. No man in history has ever broken out of it." Then I let them twist around for a while and gradually I let them slide out and say I "Good God, the first man in history ever to work his way out of the Double Reverse Panther Bear Pretzel Twist! Congratulations."

(SHE *has made no effort to get out, stays twisted*)

MISS JANUS: But I can't get out.

(HAROLD *kisses* MISS JANUS *awkwardly, then ardently, then tenderly*)

HAROLD (*Setting her down*): Look, that isn't why I told you about the game. I wasn't working around to that, or anything.

MISS JANUS: It's a lovely game.

HAROLD: The kids love it. They can play it with me for hours. (*As as afterthought*) Listen, what kind of a kiss was that? I just don't know how good I'd be at kissing under the circumstances.

MISS JANUS: It was delicious. Listen, I don't want you to get the wrong idea. I've done an awful lot of drifting in and out of things, but actually I've only really had one all-out start-to-finish love thing. A writer. We were both very new with each other. What we did was wander through each other like we were the first man and woman. The sex part with him was always very quick, almost instantaneous. It was very sad. We're still friends. He married a girl who's as quick as he is—and he says they're very happy.

HAROLD: Maybe I'll get through the night. I've got this great fighting chance . . . I once read a novel about a guy who just got divorced and what he did to get through was a lot of physical activity. Push-ups. Every morning he'd get up, light a fire, and start doing push-ups. I wonder if I ought to try a few. (*Gets down on the floor and begins doing push-ups, gets up to around ten*) You know, it's not bad at all. I wonder how deep knee bends would be. (*Does a few*) Hey, you know it's really something. I'll be goddamned if it doesn't help. (*Starts to do an isometric exercise*) I'll probably come up with a hernia.

MISS JANUS: Hercules had a hernia.

HAROLD: Hercules? How'd you find that out?

MISS JANUS: I saw a statue of him in the Louvre and there was a funny little hernia line nobody else noticed. I once told a boy I had a hernia. At college. He drove me out to a lake and asked me how I'd feel about some heavy petting. It sounded so *heavy*. So I told him I had a hernia . . . Listen, would you like a massage?

HAROLD (*With irony*): Yeah, that's exactly what I'm in the mood for. I'm supposed to drift into a little massage . . .

MISS JANUS: You know, a lot of people believe it's a homosexual thing. I don't. But I don't even believe homosexual relations really exist. Certainly not between two men. Why would they bother? There are so many other things they could be out doing. I don't think it's ever really happened. Maybe in Germany once or twice, in the thirties, but that was the only time. I think it's something some-

one made up to play a big joke on society. A couple of fags
made it up.

HAROLD: You know, for a second I thought that frogman
was a fag. He's probably been keeping it up his sleeve. I
just remembered something about the way he slithered
into the water after that fish. (*Reflecting*) That's all I'd
need. Losing my wife to a goddamned fag. (*Quiet, desperate anger*) Boy, if I ever found that out, then I'd *really*
break his head. . . . (*In a different mood*) I'm not sure
I want to know, but where'd you learn about massages?

MISS JANUS: My father taught me how to do them. I thought
it would be incestuous, but it really isn't. It just feels good.

HAROLD: How do you know it's not incestuous?

MISS JANUS: With my *father*?

HAROLD: What do I do?

MISS JANUS: Roll up your pants.

HAROLD: What do you mean?

MISS JANUS: I want to do your knees.

HAROLD: What good's that going to do?

MISS JANUS: You'll see.

(HAROLD *rolls up his pants*)

They're very attractive.

HAROLD: Thank you.

(SHE *begins to massage his knees*)

MISS JANUS (*Still massaging*): I bet you were good in sports too.

HAROLD: I was about average. But I always had great form. (*Demonstrating with scythe*) I'd pick up a tennis racket or start fooling around with a basketball and I'd make these sly little moves and these great championship faces and they'd think God knows what was coming. I did a lot of losing, but it didn't seem to matter. (*Responding to massage*) Hey, you know, you're right, it *is* good. Of all things, I never even knew I *had* knees before and yet here they are, out of the clear blue skies, feeling great.

MISS JANUS: I believe some people have a special touch, don't you? That young man in the French movie who all he has to do is touch this girl on the wrist at a party and she moves right out on her millionaire husband and goes to live with him in a little cellar somewhere. And it all started with a touch.

HAROLD (*Pushing HER off*): I'd like to make a little announcement about my knees. My knees have just become the greatest knees in town. Everyone said they were finished, washed up, that they'd never work again. Well, you've put them back on their feet. I want to thank you for giving them another break in show business. (THEY *shake hands*) But she never showed up, did she? And nothing's really changed, has it? . . . Dr. Schoenfeld. (HE *picks up phone, dials*) Dr. Schoenfeld?

(*Cut-out of* DR. SCHOENFELD *appears*)

DR. SCHOENFELD'S VOICE: Speaking . . .

HAROLD: Surprise. This is Harold Wonder. I'm in Cap Ferrat.

DR. SCHOENFELD'S VOICE: All right, if you want to be in France. I didn't realize you knew I was here.

HAROLD: Oh sure. Don't you remember? In that haberdashery store? We were both trying on bathrobes. Look, I'm in terrible trouble and I'm just calling up guys. But this isn't just a call. I really have to ask you to come over here. You can make it in about twenty minutes. Look, obviously you don't have to come . . .

DR. SCHOENFELD'S VOICE: What's the difficulty, Harold?

HAROLD: The difficulty is that I'm climbing up the walls. It's the kind of thing you'd never get into in a million years. It's my wife. She's out with this goddamned spade frogman and I think she's going to stay the whole night. It's that whole night thing that scares me.

DR. SCHOENFELD'S VOICE: Harold, isn't the frogman just one chapter?

HAROLD: One chapter? Oh yeah, and I've been turning him into the whole Modern Library. Look, Dr. Schoenfeld, I don't want to appear ungrateful, but that capsule style just isn't enough this time. Can you come over? I've tried everything. A little while ago I started to shake. I'm afraid I'm going to blow sky high. I don't want the kids to see me that way. So could you please try to make a run over here? Please.

DR. SCHOENFELD'S VOICE: Harold, you know what your problem is—you're good at looking up and down but you've never once looked at life sideways.

HAROLD: Look, Doc, I don't want sideways now. Will you don't give me sideways.

DR. SCHOENFELD'S VOICE: No sideways, eh?

HAROLD: No. I really need you. Could you sort of come over and spend the night. I really need somebody I can depend on.

DR. SCHOENFELD'S VOICE: Well, Harold, I have a friend visiting.

HAROLD: There's plenty of room. Bring your friend along. I really do need you, right this second. (HE *hangs up*)

(DR. SCHOENFELD's *cut-out disappears*)

He'll be here. I know it. If it was me and I heard a guy who sounded like I did, I'd be over in a flash. . . . You know, right this second, as we sit here, my wife is up on a chandelier with a spade.

MISS JANUS: You like the way that sounds, don't you?

HAROLD: What do you mean? Spade? I guess so. Spade. It comes out so smooth. They have all the good names. (*Enunciating very deliberately*) Coon. Shine. All those n's. Wop. Kike. See? Nothing. If you ask me, I think she picked one of them just to confuse me. Or to prove something to me. She knows how mixed up I am about colored guys. There's just no right way to be about Negroes. I went down to that Freedom March a couple of years ago in Washington. All of a sudden. Actually I knew I was going, but I like to tell it as though I made up my mind on the spur of the moment. Makes me sound like more of a sympathizer. Anyway, I got down there and when the marching started it got kind of crowded and a man fainted. I stopped to see if I could help and a huge Negro in back twisted my arm up behind me and said "Pass 'em by, pass 'em by." He kept walking me that way till we got way the hell out in a field some-where. And he's still saying, "Pass 'em right up, pass 'em by." Finally I said "I passed the son of a bitch by already," but he just kept marching me along saying "You ain't really passed him all the way by yet." He finally let me go, I don't know where, someplace in Baltimore. That didn't exactly put me in the right mood for a Freedom March. I got to listen to some of the speeches anyhow—they've really got some wonderful speakers, guys you've never heard of who can knock you out of your seat.

MISS JANUS: And then something terrible happened, right?

HAROLD: You ready?

MISS JANUS: Clunk. (SHE does a fastening thing at her waist, then explains) Safety belt.

HAROLD: Well, I'm listening to the Reverend and he's really going to town. All goose bumps, really nailing the thing down, right in front of the Lincoln Memorial, the most stirring thing you ever heard. About a third of the way through I start to look at this little colored Freedom Marcher type. She had one of those behinds you can bal-ance things on. I couldn't take my eyes off her. I felt rotten—right in the middle of this stirring thing and I can't get my eyes off her ass. So I kind of get close to her and before long we start kidding around—in whispers— and next thing you know I've got her behind a tree. I couldn't stop myself. She was a little laundress girl from Delaware who came down by bus—her name was Eurethra —we didn't talk much. Anyway, what I'm leading up to is right through this Reverend's speech—one of the most brilliant addresses ever given—I read it next day in the *Times*—there we were, me and Eurethra behind the tree. Hell, maybe it was her fault as much as mine. I mean she was the colored one, *she* really should have been listening. I mean, what kind of guy does such a thing?

MISS JANUS: A very warm, glandular human being.

HAROLD: That'll be the day. (*Goes to shutters and cries out*) Jeannie . . . (*Then changes his mind*) I'm not going to do that any more. Listen, what do you want anyway? You enjoy listening to a messed-up guy?

MISS JANUS: I don't know what I want. Right now I'd settle for a guarantee that I'm never going to be hairy.

HAROLD: Hairy!

MISS JANUS: Like Janine Harper, a girl in my home town. She was a beautiful redheaded girl and then one summer she got very hairy. Turned into Neanderthal man right there before everyone's eyes. She cleared up in the fall and I guess she's all right now—I hear she married an optometrist—but I never got over it. If I could just be sure that'll never happen to me. If I could have a written certificate, something I could carry around. I just don't want to have to spend a hairy summer.

HAROLD: Well *I'll* guarantee it. It'll never happen to you. Never in a million years.

MISS JANUS: And I've decided that I'd like to go to bed with you.

HAROLD: Me, you'd like to go to bed with? Oh you crazy kid.

MISS JANUS: Listen, your wife has raced off with another man and you can't adjust to it. That's not an everyday thing you know. It's not as though you were carrying on about urban renewal. Besides, I'd like to see what it would be like. With many men you just know, but with you . . .

HAROLD: I'll tell you what it's like. With me, it's a one-handed number. (*Changing tones*) That black bastard told us he's got beautiful paintings on the wall. I can just about imagine. I can just picture the colored shit he's got hanging up there. Haven't you heard? That's where Picasso is having all his shows these days. At that spade's apartment. The second Picasso knocks off a canvas he rushes it over there, special delivery. It's the only place he'll show his paintings. Maybe he likes the colored smell up there; it really brings out the values. (*Phone rings.* HE *looks at her apologetically, lets it ring, goes to phone, looks back and then takes it near a clothing closet, where, standing up,* HE *begins to pull coats over his head for privacy*) Hello, Jeannie-and-if-it-is-don't-say-a-word-because-I'm-doing-all-the-talking. Now, Jeannie, look, I don't care what's happened. You got a little nervous, it's a foreign

country, all right, I'm a little shook up, but it's over,
I forgive you, and you're coming right the hell home
where you belong. We'll take a few trips. Remember, we
were going to use this as home base and see Barcelona?
. . . It is *not* just the beginning! . . . All right then, we'll
go to Liverpool. Any place you say. . . . I'm the one who
is facing facts! . . . Jeannie, I'm all alone here. What do
you think this has been like for me? . . . A *strain?* . . .
You're holed up with a nigger frogman and you call me
up and all it is is a little strain . . . Strain? (*Goes to window, yells*) I'll give you a strain, you fuckin' Mau-Mau.
I'll strain your ass. (*Back to phone*) I'm not trying to put
him down. . . . All right, all right. . . . Okay, he *is*. He's
very nice. Nicer than I'll ever be. . . . Listen, I've been
plenty nice. In my own style. . . . I use both hands too!
It was just that one time. I can't explain it. (*Hardening*)
Now listen, Jeannie, you get your tail the hell back here
or I'm throwing you right the hell out of the house. You
hear? I don't care if you're impressed or not. . . . All right,
you're out. You hear that? I've thrown you out of the
house. . . . I don't have to have you here to throw out of
the house. You're out. (*Pacifying*) All right, Jeannie, I
know. I'm sorry. Okay, if you say it's real—you say it's
honest—then that's what it is. That's right, baby, with us
it was filth and with your new friend it's purity all the way.
. . . I know. . . . Uh-huh. That's right, baby. Will you put
your clothes on now and get your white ass over here.
What do you have to do, get one more of those spade
screws? One more of those little screwba dewbas? Got to
feel those Freedom Flippers around your toochis one more
time? . . . Jeannie, I can't make it through the night . . .
Jeannie, you're not home in an hour, I swear to Christ
I'm walking the hell out of here. . . . I don't give a shit
about the kids. . . . That's how I feel about it. I don't see

you in the doorway, I'm walking right the hell out of here into the French night. . . . You just try me. . . . (*Soft*) Jeannie, do you remember Quebec? All right, forget Quebec. I'll never mention it again. I mean just come home. Will you just do that. . . . He won't *let* you? (*Out the window*) You won't let her, you fag bastard. I just heard about that. It just came in over the wire. What do you mean, you won't let her? You open those goddamned doors or I'm coming over there to cut your balls off. (*To the phone*) All right, I'm calm. . . . I am . . . It's because you can't see me. I'm in complete control of myself.

(THIEF *enters, pot on his head, and begins to steal things.* HAROLD *doesn't see him.* MISS JANUS *tries to warn* HAROLD, *then to reason with* THIEF)

(HAROLD *shouts out the window*): You like my billboards, eh. I'll give you billboards. I'll billboard your ass when I get hold of you, you black son of a bitch. (*Into phone at same time he spots* THIEF) Yeah, well he can afford to be a gentleman. I'll show him dignity. I'll show him who's beneath who. Now, Jeannie, will you just come home. (*Hollering out window, ignoring* THIEF) You went one step too far. A lot of guys make that mistake with me. (*To* THIEF) Hold on a second. (*Into phone*) Hold on a second. (*Picks up scythe and as* THIEF *leaps through window hurls it after* HIM *through the shutters, then plumps down in a chair, addressing* MISS JANUS *with great casualness*) She'll be here in twenty minutes flat. Have I steered you wrong once tonight?

(BOTH *watch curtain come down*)

CURTAIN

ACT TWO

ACT II

(*The action continues directly from Act I*)

MISS JANUS: You were wonderful. I never saw anyone move that fast.

HAROLD: I love action. That's the one thing I'm crazy about.

(*Door knock*)

That's my wife. I know her knock.

(GENDARME *enters holding* THIEF's *arm with one hand, scythe with the other*)

GENDARME: I'm sure you must have some explanation, monsieur.

HAROLD: Hey, you got him! That's great!

GENDARME (*Taking out notebook*): Just because you Americans have everything and we have nothing does not mean you can make fun of me.

HAROLD: Who's making fun? Where's the fun? (*To* MISS JANUS) Was I just making fun of him?

GENDARME: Never mind. Do not take that superior tone with me. And then as soon as I leave, the sly little jokes will

begin. Just because you have your washing machines and
your General Motors.

HAROLD: Look, I don't want to go into a whole thing. Will
you just book this guy and get him the hell out of here.

THIEF: All men are thieves.

GENDARME: He is not entirely wrong, you know. I arrive here,
you expect me to fall at your foot, to lick your boot. France
is a proud nation, monsieur, something you and your General Motors will never understand. (*Pauses*) What is the
salary of the American policeman?

MISS JANUS: Sixty-three hundred dollars a year. (HAROLD *is
astonished*) It was in *U.S. News and World Report.* I
just happen to remember.

GENDARME (*to* THIEF): I, Pierre Luclos, am paid forty-two
francs a week and on top of that, these Americans come
here and throw shit in my face!

HAROLD (*Imitating Jack Benny*): Now wait a minute!

(LANDLADY *enters*)

LANDLADY (*Surveying scene*): It has not happened here. I
saw nothing. It did not occur in my house. Oh, perhaps
once, when the Russians were having their Yalta confer-
ence in the attic. They are terrible, the Russians. You know
how long I know the Khrushchev boys? I would never have
them in my house again.

HAROLD: Tonight I'm getting Yalta? I need a little Yalta?

GENDARME: Hold the horse, monsieur. I am not one of your Negroes that you can trample . . .

HAROLD: Listen, that problem is not quite as bad as it sounds. Some of them are doing pretty well. Pretty goddamned well.

THIEF: All men are thieves. The butcher is a thief. The baker. The honest man who works at the same job for forty years, from nine to six, goes home each night to his family and never steals a dime. What is he, a thief. He is cheating his loved ones. He is cheating his destiny. He is a lowly rotten scum of a thief, the worst of them all. There you have philosophy.

HAROLD: There you have garbage. (*To* GENDARME) Are you going to lock this guy up or am I supposed to wait till he kills a few of my kids.

GENDARME: When I am ready, monsieur, and only when I am ready. (*Paces the room elaborately*) The charges, Mr. Yankee Doodle?

HAROLD: What do I know about French charges? Ask him why he wears that pot while you're at it.

THIEF: Decadence, sir. A symbol of your rotten, bourgeois Western decadence.

> (GENDARME, *choked with emotion, begins to sing* "La Marseillaise." THIEF, LANDLADY *and* MISS JANUS *join him while baffled* HAROLD *looks on*)

GENDARME: Come, my friends. We have taken enough from this man.

THIEF (*Banging pot on his head*): All men are thieves. Murderers, liars and pederasts too. I offer you philosophy.

(THIEF, GENDARME, LANDLADY *exit, all singing "La Marseillaise."* DR. SCHOENFELD *enters. He appears to have weekend baggage with him. He is dressed, atypically, in a very flashy manner*)

HAROLD: Dr. Schoenfeld! What a pleasure. Let me take your bags. It's amazing, I feel better already.

DR. SCHOENFELD: Good evening, Harold.

HAROLD: Didn't you bring your friend?

(*Wild-looking blonde appears. This is* CHEYENNE)

CHEYENNE: Here I am, love. 'Ello there. Say, Phillsy told me about your wife. Never you mind. Soon as she runs out of money that spade'll drop her like a hot pizza.

HAROLD: Good Christ!

SCHOENFELD: Harold, I'd like you to meet Cheyenne. (*Noticing* MISS JANUS) I don't think I've had the pleasure.

MISS JANUS: Hi, Dr. Schoenfeld, I'm Carol Janus.

CHEYENNE: 'Ello lamb chop, how are you?

HAROLD (*Privately, to* SCHOENFELD): This is the fancy treatment you thought up? My wife's out screwing the rules committee of SNICK and you had to come running over here with this?

SCHOENFELD: It's just one chapter.

CHEYENNE (At bookshelves): Say, you got any books by Bernie Malamud? Once you get started on those urban Jews it's like eating potato chips. If you ask me, you can take C. P. Snow and shove him up your keester.

SCHOENFELD: Cheyenne, please. I have something important to say to Mr. Wonder. (Beckoning HAROLD toward couch. MISS JANUS, CHEYENNE sit on couch, too) Harold, it's become obvious that we can't work with sideways any longer. Perhaps it's time we looked into our relationship. Now, I agree we've had some good times in the haberdashery store. But you know, you've never really taken our talks seriously. Do you know why, Harold? Because they've never really cost you anything.

HAROLD: Cost me anything . . .

MISS JANUS: Oh sure, it's just like figs. You know how delicious they are. But imagine, if you had all the figs in the world, they just wouldn't be delicious any more.

HAROLD: Look, hold the figs. Go ahead, Dr. Schoenfeld.

SCHOENFELD: Your friend is right. What I want you to do, before we go any further, is to give me something valuable —not money—but something you really treasure. Then I'm convinced you'll listen to me.

CHEYENNE (With pride, to MISS JANUS) He's my shrink, you know.

HAROLD (Looking around): Something valuable . . . what kind of valuable?

MISS JANUS: I didn't know they dated patients.

(HAROLD *exits in his search*)

CHEYENNE (*To* MISS JANUS): We don't start the couch bit until after the fall. This is sort of a trial period. Like exhibition baseball. Say, you've got an honest face. Shall I tell you what my problem is? Sexual climaxes.

MISS JANUS: You poor thing.

CHEYENNE: No, no, I have too many of them. He's going to try to cut me down to just five a night.

MISS JANUS: Oh, that should be plenty.

(HAROLD *returns*)

HAROLD: All I could find was this muffler. My mom knitted it for me when I was around ten. There was a deaf kid who tried to take it away from me once. A strong deaf kid. A deaf bully. I had to hit him right in the mouth. It was no fun hitting a deaf guy, believe me. But it was worth it. I got it back and I've kept it ever since.

DR. SCHOENFELD: Now you're really sure you care about this muffler?

HAROLD: I really do.

DR. SCHOENFELD: All right, give me the muffler. Now, Harold, listen very carefully. When I was in the Army, I was in grain supply. As a matter of fact, I was the officer in charge of purchasing barley for the entire states of Kansas and

Oklahoma. Now barley, God bless it, as we all know, gets very damp. And damp barley means only one thing—trouble—not for the barley, but for the barley personnel. Well, sure enough, I soon came down with a respiratory ailment. Now, the Army doctors were convinced it was a rare disease common only to barley workers. Do you know what it turned out to be, Harold? It wasn't a barley disease at all. It was bronchitis. . . . Harold, do you see what I'm getting at?

HAROLD (*Muses awhile*): Give me back the muffler.

DR. SCHOENFELD: You're not getting the muffler back.

HAROLD: Come on, hand it over.

DR. SCHOENFELD: No, Harold.

HAROLD: Give me the goddamned muffler.

> (*Tug of war follows, with* MISS JANUS *and* CHEYENNE *joining in.* HAROLD *gets muffler back*)

HAROLD (*Winding muffler around his neck*): Y'ain't getting the muffler. Not for barley. I was better off with sideways.

DR. SCHOENFELD (*Collecting himself, gathering dignity*): Well, Harold, it's a little late. Perhaps in the morning you'll see things differently. (*Standing beside* CHEYENNE) And now, if you'll show us to my room . . . (*Gathers luggage*)

HAROLD: Room? Yeah, that's right, I forgot. All right, go ahead. Go upstairs. Take a left at the top. Make sure it's a left. I got my kids up there.

MISS JANUS: Good night, Dr. Schoenfeld. 'Night, Cheyenne.

CHEYENNE: Nighty night, all.

DR. SCHOENFELD (*At top of stairs*): I don't need his muffler. It was for his own good.

CHEYENNE: C'mon love, let's have a go. (THEY *enter bedroom*)

HAROLD: How long have I known that guy? Now he's giving me barley.

MISS JANUS: He really let you down, didn't he?

HAROLD: No, it just seems that way, to the untutored eye.

MISS JANUS: Maybe you'd like to hear about my obscene phone call.

HAROLD: Nope. I don't know much tonight, but that's one thing I'm sure of, that I don't want to hear about your obscene phone call. Maybe when this whole thing dies down we can meet somewhere and you can tell me about it. At some little French place. I just know I'm not up to it tonight. . . . How obscene was it?

MISS JANUS: That's the whole point. It was the most timid obscene call in the world. It was from a boy at Columbia. He was studying library management and I think he'd been reading Henry Miller. He called me from the stacks. It was the shyest obscene phone call. So I asked him to meet me in the school cafeteria . . .

(CHEYENNE *appears in robe*)

CHEYENNE: Listen, is there a crapper in this joint?

HAROLD (Gesturing): Oh man.

CHEYENNE (Walking toward indicated room): I hope it has a bidet. I've been all over France and I'm the only one who hasn't seen one yet. I'm not even sure I'm looking for the right thing. (Disappears in room)

HAROLD: Why'd you have to meet him? Why'd you have to meet him and then come here to France and tell me about it with what I'm going through? Why didn't you just hang up?

MISS JANUS: His face was practically all horn-rimmed glasses. I talked to him for hours. It was his first obscene phone call, just like it was mine. We went up to my room for a while . . .

HAROLD: All right, all right, hold the punchline. I knew I didn't want to hear this one. And I was right.

(CHEYENNE appears in underwear, soaked)

CHEYENNE: Well, I'll be goddamned. So that's how it works. You'd think they'd at least have directions on the little stinker. (She goes back into the bedroom)

HAROLD: Why didn't you call the police? That's what you're supposed to do. If everyone just invited perverts over to the house for tea like that what the hell kind of a world would it be? . . . Probably wouldn't be that bad. (Reflecting) Jesus, I just remembered. I made one of those calls myself.

MISS JANUS: Listen, more people than you think . . .

HAROLD: No, I was just a kid. I had a crush on a teacher named Miss Baines, so I looked up this word in the dictionary and I said it to her. "Hello, Miss Baines," I said. "Yes," she answered. "Pelvis," I said, and then I slammed down the phone. I think she knew though. Every time I got up to recite, she put on this pelvic expression. That's something to remember, here in France, years later, and my wife's on a trapeze with the Brown Bomber . . .

(CHEYENNE *comes downstairs humming, semi-nude*)

CHEYENNE: Hi. Phillsy likes to have a little warm milk before he gets rolling. Helps him crank up his motor. Y'know, I knew a bloke once who liked me to cover him up from head to toe with mayonnaise. Poor bastard. It was the only way he could get his rocks off. (CHEYENNE, *erupting in vulgar laughter, enters kitchen*)

HAROLD: You want to know something *really* awful?

MISS JANUS: What's that?

HAROLD: I think I know where to find them.

MISS JANUS: Your wife?

HAROLD: Remember her? That's really something to have to come right out and admit. Eleven Rue Domergue—he said it one night and it stuck with me. So how come I'm not going anywhere? How come I'm just hollering out of windows?

MISS JANUS: You're just not ready.

HAROLD: When do I get ready? When she moves to the Congo?

(CHEYENNE *comes out of kitchen, whistling. Goes back into bedroom*)

MISS JANUS (*Stretching*): You know, it isn't that much. . . . We could just sort of drift upstairs too . . .

HAROLD (*Getting up*): I don't know how it would be. . . . Maybe if you just told me a few more of those stories. Do you have any left? Just feed me a few more and we'll see what happens.

MISS JANUS: All right. (SHE *comes toward him, sits behind him*) Once I was trying on dresses in a store up in Maine. I reached into the size nine rack and there was a little man all covered up inside a two-piece jersey ensemble . . .

> (*Light changes as though many hours have passed. Indication is that it is dawn.* HAROLD *is still in his bathrobe, groggy, exhausted.* MISS JANUS *has been going on with her stories, as though* SHE *has been telling them endlessly*)

. . . a Russian take-out restaurant. Anyway, I was delivering an order of borscht to a customer and I see his pockets are all filled with petitions, bills, proclamations. So I put two and two together and I said "Listen, just because you're in the House of Representatives doesn't mean I'm staying over tonight." (*Realizes how much time has gone by*) Oh my God, I locked Nero and Abby out.

> (SHE *exits.* MRS. WONDER *appears. Young, early thirties, attractive, rather forlorn at the moment, and prone to bumping into things. She is gentle in manner*)

JEAN WONDER: Harold . . . How are you? . . .

HAROLD: What do I know? . . .

JEAN: How are the kids?

HAROLD: They're fine, under the circumstances. You all right?

JEAN: Pretty good. My arm hurts though.

HAROLD: What happened?

JEAN: I think I got gas in it.

HAROLD: What do you mean gas? You can't have gas in your arm.

JEAN: No, that's what it is. I'm sure of it. Somehow it curled around through here and up around here and got right into my arm. It'll be all right.

HAROLD: It's not gas. Remember that party? What was it, Friends of the Middle East? You were positive you were having a heart attack. *That* was gas.

JEAN: That was a small heart attack, Harold. I just accepted it and when it was over I was grateful and that was the end of it.

HAROLD: Everything else all right?

JEAN: My neck is a little tensed up. I'm just going to have to live with that. (SHE *starts to dust*) You okay?

HAROLD: Jeannie, don't dust now, will you.

JEAN: Well, what am I supposed to do, leave it there, just let it accumulate? Breathe it all in? Foreign dust. How do we know what's in it?

HAROLD: There's nothing in it. It's just a little French dust. No dusting now, okay? Will you do me that favor. I'm trying to get a little sore. There's something that happens to your shoulders—when you dust—and I don't want to get involved in that now. They get frail or something. I probably never told you, but I can't stand to see you dust. It's like I took this young, fragrant, hopeful, beautiful young girl and turned her into an old cleaning lady.

JEAN: Women like to dust, silly. It doesn't hurt them.

HAROLD: Well it hurts the hell out of me. I can't stand it.

    (SHE *stops dusting*)

JEAN: How about you? In your bathrobe. I can stand that? And making that face at me . . .

HAROLD: Which one's that?

JEAN: You know which one. There's only one. You made it at Gloria Novak's wedding reception, the first time I ever saw you. At the salad table. I looked up from my salad and I see this big guy making a face at me.

HAROLD: I don't know what you're talking about.

JEAN: Not much. That little boy face. Whenever you want something. Look at you. You can't even switch off to another one, even right now. You did it to me then and you're doing it right now.

HAROLD: What I'm doing right this second, right now?

JEAN: That's right.

HAROLD: I never made this face before in my life.

JEAN: Right. I just came in here . . . I was going to get a few things . . . (*Starts for bedroom*)

HAROLD (*Intercepting her*): No things, no things. That's one line I never want to hear. (*In British accent*) "Dudley, I've come for my things." Anybody gets their things, that's the end of their things. In this house you get your *stuff*, hear? And you don't get that either. . . . This is some mess.

JEAN: I know.

HAROLD: I think this is the worst we ever had.

JEAN: I don't know, Harold. I think when I was pregnant and we couldn't get any heat in the apartment and you had to organize a warmth committee in the building at four in the morning. I think that was worse.

HAROLD: No, I think this is worse. I had a lot of people on my side in that one. I had the whole building cheering me on. I'm all alone on this one.

JEAN: What kind of alone? You think I'm loving this? That I'm loving every second of it . . .

HAROLD: You're loving it more than I am. Anybody'd be loving it more than I am. There's not one person I can think of who wouldn't be loving this more than I am. . . . You think we'll get out of it?

JEAN: I don't know, Harold. At this point I'd settle for just getting through the morning.

HAROLD (*On his knees, cracking*): Ah come on, Pidge, will you just quit it right now. Will you get the hell back home. Will you just stay here. What do you want to do, ship me off to Happydale? I'm down here on the floor. I'm not a guy who does that.

JEAN (*Comforting*): I know, Harold, I know.

HAROLD (*Recovering slightly*): Look, there's just one thing I have to find out. This is important. Did you get into things like Pidge? Does he know I call you Pidge?

JEAN: That's what you consider important? That's what this is all about to you? Pidge?

HAROLD: No, seriously, I just have to know that one thing and then I'll never bother you again.

JEAN: I may have said something . . .

HAROLD (*Leaping up in triumph*): You told him Pidge. That's probably the first thing you blurted out. I was just on the floor where I've never been in my life—and you had to tell him Pidge. I was just hoping you'd keep one thing separate, one little private area so that maybe we could start battling our way back, inch by inch, to being a little bit together again. What you did is just fork it right over . . .

JEAN: I don't remember if I told him . . .

HAROLD (*Not hearing her*): All right, number one, cancel what I just did on the floor. And number two, drag in that chocolate shithead. I've been waiting for this all night.

JEAN: Harold, could you try to be a little dignified. I can get that style from my father. I don't need it from you. I grew up with that. You know, for a second I really felt a little something—the first time in years—and then you have just heaved it right out the window.

HAROLD (*Peering through window*): Is he out there?

JEAN: Yes, he's out there, Harold. But you can't see him because it's still a little dark and he has all this natural camouflage.

HAROLD (*Still looking out*): Very funny. How come he's afraid to get his black ass in here?

JEAN: He couldn't possibly face you, Harold. Not after what I told him. You see, I told him about your poise. About your quiet dignity. About your finesse in handling difficult situations. He wouldn't come within ten miles of the place.

HAROLD: I'm going to be dignified. I'm going to be Dag Fucking Hammarskjold. Just get the son of a bitch in here.

JEAN: Harold, will you just listen for a second. I'm not going to ask for your full attention because I know I'm not entitled to that. Not in the short span of time that's been allotted to me on earth. But will you listen a little. I've been outside . . .

HAROLD: I don't know you've been outside? I don't have it engraved in my brain for all time—that you've been out there?

JEAN: All right, you know I've been outside, Harold. But what you don't know is that I looked around a little. And I saw what they're doing out there. They're not hollering out of windows, Harold. They're not taking their families three thousand miles to a beautiful new country with dozens of charming little villages to roam around in—so they can stand around in bathrobes and shout things out of windows. And never see those charming villages.

HAROLD: Look, you want to know the truth? I've been trying not to say this, but you're forcing it out of me. All right, here it comes. I just don't happen to think those villages are charming. You want me to say they're charming, all right, they're charming. You got what you want. But they're not that goddamned charming. They *act* charming. No one's ever questioned it before, so they get away with it. You take Lexington Avenue and fix it up a little and you've got the same charm. And it didn't cost you thirty grand to get over here.

JEAN: Harold, let's face it. We both know there's only one charming thing in the world. You . . . in your bathrobe . . . shouting out of windows. That's the entire list. The charm lineup of our generation. . . . Let me tell you what happens to me when I'm outside, Harold. The strangest thing. You know how I trip a lot and bang my head on things and we both think it's cute, although actually it's very serious and some of the injuries will probably turn malignant at a future date—Well I don't trip over things out there. I didn't bang myself on the head once.

HAROLD: You were supposed to get your eyes checked, Jeannie. What happened to that? Is that what you were doing out there in the bushes—with that spade—getting your eyes checked?

JEAN: There's nothing wrong with my eyes, Harold. I wish it were that. If it were an eye problem, believe me, I'd grab it. No, there's a reason that women out there don't bang into things and kill themselves. You see, they've had a breakthrough out there, Harold. They actually—and you'd better sit down for this one—they actually believe there's a difference between men and women. And here's the shocker of the year. You ready? They're doing something about it. They've come up with a separate way of treating women. They speak a little more gently to them. They actually say things to women. Romantic things. And it doesn't make them feel like Herbert Marshall either.

HAROLD: Look, Jeannie, we've talked about this . . . Once and for all, I can't say "Your eyes are like deep pools" unless I really believe they are a little like deep pools. Even then I can't say it.

JEAN: They don't have that trouble, Harold. They say things that are beyond your wildest imaginings. Do you know they even recite poetry to women.

HAROLD: That miserable two-bit coon recites poetry . . . All right, get him in here.

(FROGMAN *in full undersea regalia enters casually,* *speargun in hand, flippers on feet.* HAROLD *walks* *through door and doesn't see him*)

HAROLD (*Shouting*): I dare you to come in here and face me (*Spots* FROGMAN) I'm sorry, I got a little confused.

FROGMAN (*In a heightened, mocking laying-it-on-thick Negro* *style. This "put-on" approach continues throughout—with* *only one exception, indicated further on*) That's all right, sweetie-baby, it's a tough scene all around. I can tell you got a lot of heart.

HAROLD: Now look, I'm cold, I'm shaky, I've been up all night. I'm not at my best in the morning. It takes me till around noon to hit my stride. To be perfectly frank, I'm a little afraid of colored people. It's a completely irrational thing. Little girls, even old ladies. I have this feeling they were all in the Golden Gloves once. You know what I mean?

FROGMAN: Let me give you a little advice, Jim. You sass an old colored lady, she gone lean back and give you the bad eye. She gone work some roots on you, babe, then you really in a shitstorm.

HAROLD: Very cute, very cute. There's just one thing. We happen to be on my turf now, you son of a bitch . . . (*Using scythe,* HAROLD *begins to square off with spear-* *gun-carrying* FROGMAN)

(SECOND NEGRO *enters, pipe-smoking, intellectual,* *quite good-looking in an aesthetic way. This is* REDDINGTON)

REDDINGTON: Hi, Pidge.

HAROLD: Pidge! Everybody knows Pidge. Who the hell is this?

REDDINGTON: Is everything all right . . . (*With glance at* HAROLD) Pidge?

JEAN: I'll just be another minute.

FROGMAN: Hey baby, you made the scene just in time. We all gonna' sit down and have some chitlins.

REDDINGTON: Cool it, Foxtrot.

HAROLD: Oh, now we're getting a little "cool it." How about a little "daddy." A little "dig," a little "daddy." Who is this guy, Jeannie?

JEAN: Harold, this is Ambrose Reddington.

HAROLD: That tells me a lot.

JEAN: Harold, I'm sorry, I really wanted to avoid this. I met Ambrose a few days ago . . . A complete accident. He was very sweet to me and I take full credit for him. Foxtrot is your idea, one hundred per cent. A Harold Wonder special. You like him, you can't live without him. I'll tell you what—pick up the phone, make a reservation and the two of you can go flying down to Rio.

HAROLD: Hilarious.

FROGMAN: Suppose I just slip into my travelin' duds . . .

HAROLD (*Threatening*): Don't push me too far, just don't push me too far. (*Recovering*) Give me a minute to adjust to this. (*Contemplates*) I can't adjust to this. (*Walks toward* REDDINGTON. *Resuming anger*) As I was just saying. (*Shouts*) We're on my turf now, you son of a bitch. We're not at any Black Muslim convention.

FROGMAN: Oh, I see where it's at.

HAROLD (*To* FROGMAN): Look, I'm sorry to have to use the racial stuff, but you'll just have to overlook it. It gives me a slight edge, but I can assure you it's got nothing to do with my true feelings. If everyone felt the way I did, you guys would have clear sailing from here on in . . . (*To* REDDINGTON, *shouting*) What's important is that I can still smell my wife on you, you bastard.

REDDINGTON: Mr. Wonder, I can see that this is a difficult situation for you, but we certainly ought to be able to deal with it as mature adults.

FROGMAN: He ain't gonna be one of them mature adults. He gonna fetch the debbil on that poor old colored man. He gonna reach around there and work some roots. Right on that poor black rascal's head. Whoooooooeeeee.

HAROLD: Very cute, very cute.

FROGMAN: Shame on you babe. Just 'cause that poor old colored man went out there in the bushes and jugged your wife a few times . . .

HAROLD: Now you watch your ass. Just because I was wrong about you doesn't mean I was wrong about you.

FROGMAN: Shame on you, man. For shame . . .

(REDDINGTON *starts to cough*)

JEAN: Oh my God, are you all right?

REDDINGTON: It'll pass. It's nothing.

JEAN (*To* HAROLD): Now look what you did.

HAROLD: What *I* did!

JEAN: You started his cough. Will you do something useful for a change? Where did we put the Cheracol?

HAROLD: Cheracol? You want me to nurse him back to health? It's in the medicine cabinet. Oh never mind, I'll get it. (*As* HE *fumbles in the drawer*) I really have to congratulate you, Jeannie. I mean a little affair is one thing. But the entire Harlem Globetrotters. That's really style.

FROGMAN: Hey, Ambrose. What'd you need this shit for? You could have stayed out there in the car.

REDDINGTON: I couldn't allow Jean to face this alone.

(HAROLD *picks up medicine bottle, carries it to* RED-DINGTON *and pours a spoonful*)

HAROLD: I'm not enjoying this, you know. I'm not enjoying it one bit. I don't even know why I'm doing it. I guess that all it amounts to really (*As* REDDINGTON *swallows medicine*) is that I'm helping a guy with a bad cough.

(LANDLADY and TOURIST enter. LANDLADY spots FROG-
MAN and runs toward him exultantly)

LANDLADY: Sidney . . . How marvelous. It is Sidney Poitier.
(Embracing HIM. Then taking in frogman get-up) You
are in a James Bond movie. I can tell . . . How come you
don't write your friend, you naughty boy?

FROGMAN: I got jammed up at the Cannes Film Festival.
Once you get up there on top, everybody wants a slice of
the action. You got producers tryin' to get tight with you.
You got them starlets . . .

LANDLADY: Ah, you rascal. (SHE has unintentionally stepped
on one of his flippers. HE points this out and she backs
away with a blush)

TOURIST: I got nothing against you people. What the hell,
a party's a party. I'd sit around with a goddamned Yugo-
slav if I had to. Wouldn't blink an eyelash. I always say,
if you keep alert you can even learn something from a
Slav. Long as that Slav understands that when the buzzer
rings I head back to my section of town and he gets up
and goes back to his Slav side of town.

HAROLD (To TOURIST): I really don't need any help from you.

FROGMAN (In mock defense of TOURIST): Hey, don't pick on
him. That's my man. Anyone mess with my man gotta
hit on me first, babe. (Confidentially, with arm around
TOURIST) You like to meet some nice colored chicks?

TOURIST: Well actually, I'm just down here for a few weeks . . .

FROGMAN: I mean some real groovy colored chicks. I don't
mean any of that street trash. Something real high class . . .

(TOURIST, *abashed, exits.* LANDLADY *follows him*)

HAROLD: Jeannie, what do you want to see, a stretcher case? A French nervous breakdown? You're going to get one, you know. I'm going to sail into one any second now.

FROGMAN: Baby, you just not getting the message. You heard about those neighborhoods that get moved in on and there's nothing you can do? You're just not facing facts. You the neighborhood in this case, babe.

REDDINGTON: Foxtrot, please. Mr. Wonder, I'm sorry that my friend feels it necessary to behave in this fashion, but if you'll permit me—I'm afraid he has made a valid point. Realistically speaking, your wife and I have formed a powerful attraction for one another. It has enormous meaning to both of us. It began quite innocently, I assure you.

HAROLD: I know about those innocent attractions. I could hear the bedsprings creaking all the way across the Mediterranean.

REDDINGTON: Mr. Wonder, that's not very groovy of you.

(LANDLADY *and* TOURIST *enter*)

TOURIST (*To* LANDLADY): I sort of like the French. It's the Italians you got to watch. The important thing is to keep them away from shiny stuff. Rings, silverware, tinfoil. Drives 'em crazy. It isn't anything they can help. Something happens, inside their heads. Any time you invite an Italian person over, make sure you don't have anything around that makes a jingling sound.

(LANDLADY and TOURIST go upstairs on inspection tour)

HAROLD: Do you actually have to handle him, Jeannie? Right in front of me. You know, if I didn't see this, maybe in thirty-three years or so I might be able to forget the thing, pretend it didn't happen. . . . Jeannie, will you do me a favor. Will you name one way in which this is helping me. One way that it's enriching my life . . .

FROGMAN: You just not taking the right attitude, man. You could clean up. I heard about this fella, he hired another guy to jug his wife and then he sold tickets to his buddies to come down and watch. You work it that way, at least you pickin' up a little cash on the deal. Tell you what. Here's my money, I'll take five tickets down front, right now . . .

TOURIST: I've been watching you awhile, Foxtrot, and I just want to say right now that I respect you as a man. You're coming through loud and clear and nasty and I can hear you. Now I'm white and you're one of those black guys, but just one man to another—me standing here, you standing way the hell over there . . .

FROGMAN: I respect you too, man. I'm going to give you something. I'm going to give you a shine. I'm gonna shine up your ass. Hey, shine 'em up, shine 'em up.

(Chases TOURIST out)

LANDLADY (Wagging finger): Sidney!

(LANDLADY exits)

HAROLD (*To* REDDINGTON): If you were a Puerto Rican I'd feel the exact same way. I'm just using every weapon I can lay my hands on.

REDDINGTON: When one's masculinity is being threatened, one often resorts to . . .

HAROLD: One? What kind of one? Who talks like that? Is that the kind of poetry he recites? One. Jeannie, you know I've followed you on a lot of this, and I admit I don't walk off with the award for the Greatest Married Fellow, but I honestly don't see the big deal about this guy.

REDDINGTON (*Reciting, in something of a counterattacking style*): "What matter cakes or wine or tasty bouillabaisse . . . When love lies bruised and clotted on the thin and punished lips of our American black dream . . ."

HAROLD: Big deal. LeRoi Jones, right?

REDDINGTON: No. I wrote it.

HAROLD: I'd like to see you get that junk published.

REDDINGTON: I've already heard from the *Partisan Review*.

HAROLD (*Panicked*): The *Partisan*? What did they say?

REDDINGTON: They were impressed by the combination of raw power and delicacy . . .

HAROLD: Hah! You don't even know a standard *Partisan* rejection . . . "Dear Sir: Despite the raw power and delicacy of your poem, we regret . . ."

REDDINGTON: No, they bought it. It's scheduled for the fall issue.

HAROLD: Oh well, the fall issue . . .

JEAN: Harold, you could learn a little from this. Instead of automatically hating it.

HAROLD: Learn? All right. I'm learning. Here's a little poetry. (*In a lisping, effete style*) "Intruders ye be . . . make haste, abandon this place . . . Or I'll punch that spade in his colored face."

REDDINGTON (*With controlled anger*): Don't push me too far, mister.

HAROLD (*To* REDDINGTON): Push you too far . . . The main thing is I can outwrite you, I can outfight you, I can outthink you . . .

FROGMAN: Yeah, but there's one thing you can't out him, babe. That man there (*With a sly, sexual gesture*) is a colored man.

REDDINGTON: Foxtrot . . .

FROGMAN: Yeah, baby.

REDDINGTON: I see no point in turning this into a gutter confrontation.

FROGMAN: Shit man, I was just holdin' up my Negritude. That man was hittin' up on you, Ambrose.

(TOURIST and LANDLADY *enter.*)

REDDINGTON: I can take care of myself.

HAROLD: Well, what the hell would you do? I mean, say you were in my shoes. Say I was you for a second and you were me.

FROGMAN: You askin' an awful lot, babe.

HAROLD: No, I'm serious. What the hell am I supposed to do? Let your friend just waltz off with her? Because he's colored. Throw in a few kids. Maybe some General Electric stock I've been saving up. To show I'm not prejudiced. You know this is not an easy position to be in. I'm just trying to hang in there. It's bad enough I'm not allowed to get as angry as I'd like. If I toss in a little racial slur every now and then, you'll just have to put up with it. If you don't like it, you know where the door is. (HE *suddenly grabs a wine bottle and smashes it on a ledge, brandishing the jagged edge toward the* GROUP, *the* NEGROES *in particular*) All right, that's it. There's no more problem because I just solved the whole thing. Anybody comes near me they get my initials carved in their head.

> (*Everyone freezes in real panic and shock as* HAROLD *grabs* JEAN, *brandishing jagged bottle with great menace*)

I can't go through with the thing. (*Flings away bottle.* FROGMAN *catches it*)

REDDINGTON (*Putting out arm*): Jean . . . It's all right, Pidge, it's all right.

FROGMAN (*To* HAROLD): You know I like that—the way you whipped out that bottle and almost cut your own natural-born ass off. I liked that, man. Little more of that, you gonna be ready for One Hundred and Twenty-fifth Street.

TOURIST: Say, you fellows aren't serious about that Black Power thing, are you?

FROGMAN: You'll be the first to know, babe. We got you right at the top of the mailing list.

(*Chases* TOURIST *out with jungle sounds and speargun*)

HAROLD: Look, Jeannie, I really don't want this happening right now. If you'd come in here last night when I was fresh, rested, enthusiastic, when I was at the top of my form, you'd have seen a whole different guy. I'd have settled this thing in two seconds flat and believe me everyone in this room would have walked out of here feeling like a complete winner. But, Jeannie, I can't operate in the morning, you know that. I haven't even settled into the day yet. I'm still in my bathrobe. You put me in a pair of slacks, you'll see a whole different scene. I don't even have my eyes open and you're throwing spades at me —a whole blizzard of spades. Spades—as far as the eye can see . . .

REDDINGTON: Mr. Wonder, please, a little self-control . . .

HAROLD: All right, all right. I just want you to know that I'm not entirely responsible. There's something about mornings. I assure you if it was last night you wouldn't have heard a single racial slur out of me. Maybe one or two, tops. (*To* REDDINGTON) Now look, you got her, all right. You sneaked in there, you read poems, you're a colored guy, you did crazy things, I don't know what you did. What-ever it was, the main thing is she's yours. For the next thirty-two years she's going to be strapped to your side. At the most maybe I'll bump into her accidentally one night, have a little drink, maybe some dinner. It'll be dif-ferent then. Neither of us will talk much, just as though we're total strangers. Maybe our fingers will touch acci-dentally, and we may even slip off to a motel together and have this exquisite evening, just as though it were chore-ographed, everything that happens just sheer magic. And then we part at dawn, a little sadly perhaps, but without any real regret.

LANDLADY (*Simultaneously with last part of* HAROLD's *roman-tic fantasy, timed so that last word of her speech and* HAROLD's *come together*): Ah, l'amour. The joy of it. The tears and the heartache. When there was only one person in the world for you. The secret meetings. The touch of a hand in the darkness. Ah, when I was a jeune fille. Floop, floop, floop.

HAROLD: Will you floop the hell out of here. Look, can I please have a couple of minutes alone with my wife? Can we empty out Grand Central for a while?

JEAN: Harold, there's nothing we can't say right out here . . .

REDDINGTON: Pidge, I think it's a reasonable request. But if you'd like me to stay here, I will.

JEAN: No. It's all right.

REDDINGTON (*Reciting in a soothing manner*): "Wait here and I'll be back, though the hours divide, and the city streets, perplexed, perverse, delay my hurrying footsteps . . ."

LANDLADY (*To* REDDINGTON. SHE *is still angered by* HAROLD's *rough words*): Take care, monsieur. Eddie Fisher has stood in this very room and played the exact same trick on Elizabeth Taylor.

(LANDLADY *exits*)

REDDINGTON: Come on, Foxtrot. (HE *enters kitchen,* FOXTROT *lingering slightly behind*)

HAROLD (*To* FOXTROT): Now look, can I just have a few minutes to wind up the marriage?

FROGMAN: You got any cornbread in the kitchen?

JEAN: Once and for all, will you stop putting him on, Foxtrot.

HAROLD: He can ask for cornbread. What's wrong with that? I don't happen to have any cornbread, but he can certainly ask for it.

FROGMAN (*Straight, no accent, serious*): I was born on a farm in Aiken, South Carolina, one of nine children, six boys and three girls. They called me Billy-boy in those days because no matter what happened, I'd just buck my way through. Once I was driving and I turned a car over, seven times, got out, kept walking to the post office. I stay close to one brother, George, who sees to it that I don't wise off. He says "Maybe you're great, but let other people find it out. Don't you tell them." I lost my father on a farm accident, and didn't care much about it one way or the other. My mom's still pretty. She won a contest designing hats and my brother told the newspapermen if any of them interviewed her he'd go after them and kill them no matter where they tried to hide. . . . I haven't got tired of the water yet. Nothing much to it. I'll just stick with it, make a few bucks, probably quit, sometime.

(HE *shuffles off*)

HAROLD: What? Boy, what a pleasure to have two seconds of peace in your own home.

JEAN: All right, Harold, what's the great thing that you had to have me all alone to tell me about?

HAROLD: C'mon, Pidge. (*Spitting*) Ptuuii. I can't even call you Pidge any more. I'll have to think up a whole new name.

JEAN: Will you stop, Harold. You're hurting my hip.

HAROLD: What do you mean? I'm not touching you.

JEAN: When you act a certain way. It goes right to my hip. I've told you that a thousand times, but you never listen.

HAROLD: All right, I promise never to say anything that'll hurt your hip. (*Soft again*) Look, Jeannie, I've seen him now. I've checked out his routine. Truthfully—what has he got? What do you want, colored? All right, here's colored. (*Breaks into an elaborate shuffling dance routine in the old Bill Robinson style*) And that's without even being colored. It's better that way. You don't have any of the headaches. You skip the aggravation. All you have is the flashy stuff.

JEAN (*Somewhat amused*): I can't laugh, Harold. It'll start the whole sinus thing and I can't afford that now.

HAROLD: Jeannie, I know the guy now. He's not in my head, he was just *in* here. I mean, what *is* he? He's colored and he coughs. Is that what you want? That's what you're giving me up for? A colored cougher.

JEAN (*Jumping up*): All right, there's one. You wanted an example—that's one, right there. The last thing you said is the kind of remark that's complete death to my hip. You might as well take a hammer and just pound on it, right here.

HAROLD: All right, all right, you made your point. I just want to sit here one more minute, quietly, and wind up the marriage. The whole marriage that I thought was like a rock and would last a thousand years—a whole British Empire of a marriage. (THEY *rest a moment, silently*) All right, what does he do?

JEAN: What do you mean?

HAROLD: You know what I mean, Jeannie. You know. He's a colored guy, he knows stuff, he does stuff, they teach him things. Give me an idea.

JEAN: Oh God. He doesn't do any one thing, Harold. People don't do one thing. It's a whole lot of things, if you must know. A whole collection of things.

HAROLD: Well what are they? Can you tell me a few?

JEAN: You're really going about this the wrong way.

HAROLD: Tell me just one—one thing.

JEAN: I can't.

HAROLD: Will you come on, one lousy thing. What do you have to lose?

JEAN: I can't do that.

HAROLD: Jeannie, for crying out loud, the marriage is down the drain. I'm sitting here, I'm a terminal marriage fellow, will you tell me one thing . . .

JEAN: He strokes my ear . . .

HAROLD (*Leaping up*): I can't do that? I can't outstroke that son of a bitch twenty times a day? I can't outearstroke him? Let me show you. (HE *fights to stroke her ear.* SHE *struggles*) There you are—stroke . . . stroke . . . stroke.

JEAN (*Throwing him off*): Harold!

HAROLD: There. All right, how was it?

JEAN: It was thrilling, Harold. It really turned me on. Can I go now?

HAROLD: A colored stroke is great, huh, but if I do the identical thing, the exact same stroke, it's nothing. A Caucasian nothing. In the dark you wouldn't have known one from the other.

JEAN: You almost pulled my ear off.

> (HAROLD *clutches her suddenly, tries to make love to her.* SHE *struggles against him*)

HAROLD: Jeannie, look, I never felt this way. I don't know what just happened to me . . . some kind of crazy new feeling . . .

JEAN: Harold, will you please . . . there are people here . . . we're not in the bathroom . . .

HAROLD (*Continuing*): I don't care where we are.

JEAN: Harold, you know I can't just do that—just leap into it . . . and you haven't said a word to me. A preliminary word . . .

HAROLD (*Stops embrace*): All right, all right . . . Jeannie . . . you've got some helluva pair of tits on you . . . (*Jumps on her again*) You want hands. A lot of hands. You couldn't live without them. Here's hands. Forty-two hands.

JEAN: Harold! (SHE *throws him off again after great struggle*)

HAROLD (*With wounded dignity*): All right, will you just go now. Will you just collect your spades and stop taking up my valuable time.

JEAN: I've been trying to, Harold. I've been trying to leave. But you've been stroking my ear.

HAROLD: Well you had your last stroke. From your old marriage. Your last broken-down, second rate, technically lousy stroke. I just want to prepare you for something, Jeannie. So you don't hear about it second hand. So you don't read about it in the *Harlem Bugle*. When you walk out of here, I'm not folding my tent . . .

JEAN: Well I don't want you to, Harold. Is that what you think would make me happy—tent-folding?

HAROLD: What you don't see is that beneath all these layers of what you consider weakness—and maybe I'll even agree with you a little there—there's another layer that you don't know anything about. It's a little weak too, but it's toughly weak. That's the strongest kind. It's a great layer that comes from way back in my family—little villages in Budapest where these peasants would ride through the village brimming over with this tough weakness. How old am I? I've still got thirty-five good years to go. I'm a young guy. I've got great knees. I've got a terrific neck. Something you never noticed.

JEAN: I've noticed it, Harold. Many is the time I've found myself just sitting and staring out of windows, thinking about your neck. I just never could put my feelings into words. Can I go now?

HAROLD: Who's keeping you? Have I said one word? All right, a parting salute. To you I'm like an old tattered issue of *National Geographic*, right? That's how you see me. Something you find in a closet. One of those terrible issues from around 1936 with all those pictures of Borneo peasant women. With those long, endless Borneo bazooms. And I remind you of one of those issues. Are we agreed on that?

JEAN: Are we agreed on *what*?

HAROLD: But we're agreed on that, right? That I'm this old discarded guy that no woman under ninety-five would take a second look at. Oh, maybe there's a girl somewhere who's come up with a rare disease, been in a few airplane wrecks, couple of oven explosions. If the thing were set up very carefully in advance, a girl like that might sit down and have a drink with me. But aside from that type, I'm dead, right? It's all over? We agreed? Okay. What if I said I could produce—voilà! right here in the middle of this French floor, before your very eyes—a young, beautiful, fascinating, non-spade-loving girl, who tells stories that if the *Partisan Review* ever knew about them they'd have a man over here with a contract by six o'clock tonight. . . . I mean *good* stories, Jeannie, I don't mean that cakes and bouillabaisse shit. All right, now you take that gorgeous girl, I don't think she's out of her teens yet—if she never saw a spade in her life she wouldn't blink an eye—you take that girl with a figure that I don't even want to get started on, a whole new kind of body for the mid-nineteen sixties, take her and imagine her in this château trying every trick in the book—and believe me, Jeannie, these new girls coming up have got plenty of new routines—this gorgeous sylphlike girl trying every trick in the book to get your husband—who supposedly doesn't know the first thing about handling ears—to get your husband into the hay with her. All right. What is that? A little fictional tidbit. A little bouillabaisse. Would you like to meet her right now?

JEAN: Did you meet her, Harold?

HAROLD: You're damned right I did.

JEAN: Well I think one member of the family is enough. (*Starts to leave*)

HAROLD (*Calls through window*): Miss Janus . . . (*Then, for* JEAN's *benefit*) Carol . . . Honey.

MISS JANUS'S VOICE: Yes?

HAROLD: Can you come over for a second? I want you to settle a little argument.

MISS JANUS'S VOICE: Be right there.

HAROLD (*To* JEAN): All right, hold still one second and you're going to see a little cornbread. You're going to see the monstrous fate that awaits your husband as soon as you take one step outside. The reason your husband has to get down on his knees and beg you not to go.

(MISS JANUS *enters*)

Voilà!

MISS JANUS: Oh hi. We had a little accident. One of Nero's sculptures fell on top of him. It's a giant carving of a dead Spanish peasant who was sitting in the stands during a bullfight and got fatally gored by accident. Nero was going to present it to the Spanish government. He was positive Franco would go wild when he heard about it.

JEAN: Is your friend all right?

MISS JANUS: Oh yes. Luckily he's on a grease kick now. He thinks that if people keep themselves greased up as much as possible, it'll help them slide by some of their problems. Anyway, we just slid him out from under the dead peasant. You must be Mrs. Wonder.

JEAN: Yes. And Harold's been reading me your dossier. You're very pretty.

MISS JANUS: He told me all about you too, Mrs. Wonder. You're very attractive. You have this sort of mid-sixties look. No matter what I do to myself I can never look that way.

JEAN: Thank you. I've been feeling kind of mid-fifties tonight. Oh my God!

MISS JANUS: Is anything wrong?

JEAN: Do you realize that I have walked this coastline from end to end looking for printed slacks like that? Did you buy them here?

MISS JANUS: In town. Right here in Cap Ferrat. Listen, do you think they fit? Tell me, really. Every time I try something on, I've got this pack of girls from Düsseldorf who swoop down and tell me I'm making the mistake of my life.

JEAN: They fit, they fit. Listen, with your figure . . .

MISS JANUS: My figure. Listen, have you looked at yourself lately? I have a marine biologist friend—if he saw you, believe me, you'd never get out of his office alive.

HAROLD: All right, time. That's it. Hold it right there. What is this, roommates at Radcliffe? It's supposed to be a tense confrontation. Where's the tense? If it can't be tense, I don't need it. I got other things to do.

(SCHOENFELD and CHEYENNE, fully dressed, with luggage, come out of bedroom and make way downstairs)

JEAN: Oh, he's been here too. My husband's friend, the Dean of American Mental Health.

MISS JANUS: Oh, I know Dr. Schoenfeld. Hi, Dr. Schoenfeld. Hi, Cheyenne.

SCHOENFELD (*Opening door*): Harold, you're on your own. I can't carry you any longer. It's time you got up on your own two feet and faked your way into the adult community.

(*Exits with* CHEYENNE. FROGMAN *comes out of kitchen*)

FROGMAN (*To* JEAN): What's shakin', baby? You 'bout ready to split? Let me call Ambrose so we can get goin'.

HAROLD (*To* MISS JANUS): My wife's interviewing gospel singers. She's got thirty more of them out in the kitchen.

MISS JANUS: He's putting me on.

FROGMAN: No, no, he ain't putting you on. (*Sings "Uncle Misery"*)

> I don't get no visits from my
> Uncle Josh or Uncle John.
> And even Uncle Andy stay away from my door.
> The only uncle who ever come aroun' ...
> Is my Uncle Misery.
>> Uncle Misery
>> Uncle Misery ...
> I didn't invite you here ...
> He say "I know son,
> I don't need no inivitation" ...

(*Stops singing, leaves* HAROLD *trapped in song and hand-clapping*) Sheeeeet ...

JEAN: Foxtrot, aren't you laying it on a little thick?

HAROLD: Don't talk to him that way, Jeannie. The man enjoys singing. Let him sing a little. What's so terrible? He's not hurting anybody. (*To* FROGMAN) C'mon let's sing it again. I love that song.

JEAN (*To* MISS JANUS): Harold, the Great Defender of the Negro, the black man's best friend. You should see him driving. Get the picture. We're in the car on the highway and a colored person in the next lane has just gotten a little too close and forced us off the highway. Harold doesn't know it was a colored person yet and so he's gotten out on the road in his traditional style and is trying to round up ten men for a firing squad. But then Harold sees it was a colored driver. And then we have our ceremony. Harold reaches into the other car and kisses the driver on both cheeks. For being a colored driver. And for being nice enough to force us off the road.

HAROLD: Boy, you sure can lay it on thick, Jeannie. Just 'cause you've got an audience. You know damned well I've straightened out plenty of colored guys. I just don't do it in front of you. I've taken on whole moving vans full of them.

JEAN: I can just about imagine.

HAROLD: I don't straighten out colored guys? You're going to stick to that, right? (*Punches* FROGMAN *in the jaw, knocking him down*) All right, there! I just straightened one out.

(MISS JANUS *hides behind a couch*)

JEAN (*Running to* FROGMAN): Good Christ, Harold . . .

(HAROLD *is dancing up and down in his bathrobe, fighter style.* TOURIST *and* LANDLADY *enter*)

TOURIST: I saw that, son. That's the only language they understand.

(HAROLD *punches* TOURIST *in jaw.* TOURIST *reels out door into* LANDLADY's *arms.* REDDINGTON *runs in from kitchen*)

REDDINGTON: What's going on here? (HE *grabs* HAROLD, *immobilizes him*) Mr. Wonder, control yourself.

HAROLD: Jesus, what the hell did I do? (*To* FROGMAN) Look, I'm really sorry. I just realized what happened. Will you accept my apologies. I honestly didn't mean to do that.

FROGMAN (*Into fake mike, imitating Joe Louis*): I want to say hello to my folks in South Carolina, I want to say hello. He hit very hard with his left hand, he very strong with his left hand. I want to say hello. And I want to say hello . . .

HAROLD: All right, cut it out.

MISS JANUS: Maybe if I massaged his shoulders . . .

HAROLD: It won't be necessary. . . . Jesus, I really handled that beautifully.

REDDINGTON: Come on, Pidge, let's go.

JEAN: I'll be back for the children.

REDDINGTON: Mr. Wonder, I've had my fill of this vulgar exhibition. I find it truly regrettable that you couldn't have accepted this in a more gentlemanly fashion. You've blown your cool, Mr. Wonder, and you are far from a credit to your race.

HAROLD: Jeannie, please, no doors, okay? No doors. I'm not fooling around any more. You leave now, you might as well sign a death certificate for me. Just fill one out and leave it over there on the couch on your way out. Jeannie, I'm about to come out with the worst thing a guy ever said in the whole history of modern recorded statements. The kind of thing that if I know I was going to be reduced to saying it, I wouldn't have even bothered growing up. Jeannie, I have to have you in the house. And you can do whatever the hell you want. Just so long as you're here. You have to have colored guys, you got 'em. Take them upstairs with you. Close the door, I'll make the goddamned beds for you. You want a trapeze, I'll set that up too. Anything you want. I just need to have you here awhile. So I can slowly build up my strength. You want to leave then, we have a whole new situation. (To NEGROES) Look, what do you guys have to lose? You're coughing your head off; you can hardly stand on your feet. Where you going to get a cab at this hour? You go upstairs with her, it's cool, it's comfortable, you got television, you got everything you want . . .

JEAN: Will somebody get me out of here. Right this second.

REDDINGTON: Jean. (JEAN takes REDDINGTON by the arm)

HAROLD (To JEAN on her way out): What did I just do? I was trying to be nice to them. Well, what am I supposed to do, throw them out on their ass? Punch them in the mouth—I did that already . . .

(JEAN *and* TWO NEGROES *exit*)

(*Calling through door*): These people haven't had it that easy, Jeannie. They haven't had any sleigh ride. We tend to forget. They've done plenty of suffering . . . (*also through door*) Jeannie! Where you going? Hey, can't you guys get your own broads? Wait till I get my hands on you . . . You black bastards . . . What the hell did I do? Did you see me make one wrong move? Did I step out of line once? She'll be back. She just needs a few days in the sun. A different kind of sun. We get crummy sun right here around the house. You sit out there for hours, you end up white as a sheet.

MISS JANUS: You know, I think you're right. I think I'm whiter than when I started.

HAROLD: What the hell am I supposed to do now? I'm a lonely guy.

MISS JANUS: Oh, it's because she's just left. I used to feel the same way at Camp Winnetkawonta in the Berkshires when my parents just dumped me there and drove off. But then as soon as I got involved in the activities—the second I got out there on the archery court . . .

HAROLD: Look, please, don't tell me archery. It's an entirely different situation. I'm some lonely guy. I've been on my own how long . . . (*Checks watch*) Look at that, four minutes, and I'm a lonely guy. Maybe if I got out of here. Listen, do you have anything on, something where I can really celebrate being this free guy? This unattached winner . . .

MISS JANUS: I told Abby and Nero I'd help them look for shells tonight. Just before it gets dark. You could come along. If you don't mind Nero being a little greasy.

HAROLD: Who minds? I'm not going to mind. Long as I get out of here. Long as I get started in my new life.

MISS JANUS: Okay, I'll tell them. I don't like to just spring things on Nero. I like to give him plenty of lead time. . . . You be okay?

HAROLD: I'll be great. I just have to get through till around three o'clock in the afternoon. If I can just do that, I'll be in the best shape of my life.

MISS JANUS: See you later.

(SHE leaves)

HAROLD (Running to window): Hey, you'll be there, won't you?

MISS JANUS (Returning): Of course.

(SHE kisses him on cheek, exits)

HAROLD: Well don't worry about it. If you can't make it, put it out of your mind. Either way is okay. (Pause. HE paces back and forth, picks up scythe, looks at it, flings it aside, can't seem to get comfortable. Recreates all activities he's tried throughout evening—calls, knee bends, etc., *everything that's worked for him*—but he cuts off each one in the middle. *Running to door, shouting*) Jeannie, I'm going out with broads—two of them. We're going to look for shells. You met one, remember? Her friend's even better-looking—there's no comparison. You see this new girl, you forget the other one's alive. . . . I'm going out with the two of them. And this greasy guy —he's coming along too. . . . (HE *turns away for an instant, then returns to window as lights dim*) Once I go looking for shells, that's the last word you'll ever hear from me. If I find out I love it, I'll throw you right out of the house. Right out of the house. You hear me, Jeannie!

(*Lights go to black*)

Right out of the Goddamned house.

CURTAIN